LOVING
LEADERSHIP

8 Powerful Techniques
that so many leaders miss

RICHARD SUMMERFIELD

Loving Leadership

First published in 2016 by

Panoma Press Ltd
48 St Vincent Drive, St Albans, Herts, AL1 5SJ, UK
info@panomapress.com
www.panomapress.com

Book design and layout by Neil Coe.

Printed on acid-free paper from managed forests.

ISBN 978-1-784520-83-0

A CIP catalogue record for this book is available from the British Library.

This book is available online and in bookstores.

Reader testimonials:

'Richard's book reflects his own highly engaging, inspiring, committed and honest approach to leading others. The eight considerations when read with your own experiences to the fore provide every reader with a chance to build a personal road map out of any dilemmas, people and organisation issues being faced by looking at themselves first. Richard has succeeded in making a very pragmatic and readable approach work, and with his contributors he has delivered a splendid compendium of leadership insight.'

Neville Pritchard, CEO of HR in Flow Ltd

'Richard's book pinpoints a global shift in leadership style that is rapidly becoming a key differentiator of organisational success – whereby showing genuine care for others through selfless behaviours is no longer a 'nice to have' or 'something to be worked on' when you have time, it is fast becoming a business imperative for any great leader of the present or future.'

Jon Lavelle, International Leadership & Negotiation Skills Trainer

'Life and leadership is a continual learning journey. Regardless of your experience as a leader this book really helps you to take an objective look at your own strengths and areas of development. Some great, simple and straightforward ideas to help you create a happy, engaged and productive working environment and become a stronger, well-balanced leader.'

Anna Blackburn, CEO of Beaverbrooks the Jewellers

Contents

CHAPTER 9: Making it Stick   177

INTRODUCTION

Who will benefit from reading this book?

My big passion is to create a better working environment for everyone, thereby giving people a greater chance of feeling happy, valued, giving their best, and reaching their full potential. This theme is at the core of the book, which I think will appeal to four main types of people:

1. Industry leaders of any type who want to be more effective and inspiring in their roles;

2. Managers who are aspiring to be future leaders and want to practise some great habits;

3. Academics and HR practitioners looking for powerful tools and excellent leadership theories based;

4. People who simply want to create better working lives for themselves and/or others.

Loving Leadership carries a deliberate double meaning – it's for people who love leadership, and also a framework for leading with love. As you will see in the book, when people truly love to lead, and focus on leading with love, you have an unbeatable combination for inspiring others.

How is this book different from others?

There are some excellent leadership theories based on academic research, but this book is based on first hand corporate reality (with scars to prove it!) from nearly 20 years of personal experience and observation of what works and what doesn't.

Furthermore, having started as very much a 'personal mission', this book has ended up being a powerful collaboration, augmented with contributions from nearly 30 of the most influential and trusted professionals that I have had the pleasure of meeting, networking with and partnering throughout my career. I am extremely lucky to have their generously shared wisdom included in every chapter, and this extra dimension to the material also sets the book apart, as it is validated and endorsed by some of the highest calibre people in the industry.

A quick summary of my background – born and bred in Berkshire near the banks of the River Thames, I went on to graduate from Durham University with a First Class Honours in Biology & Psychology in 1996. My first job was on the Barclays Graduate Programme (well, more accurately, processing cheques in the Machine Room of a busy branch in Reading). Since then, I have worked as an HR professional for five companies across banking, insurance, professional services and IT/telecoms sectors, all of which has given me depth and breadth in every aspect of leadership. I love my career choice as an HR leader, Board Member and Company Ambassador, and have intently observed things that work well in the field of leadership and people management over the years.

I believe that leadership is at its most powerful when robust theory is partnered with hands-on experience, but I would be cautious about using one without the other. To put this into a business context, seeking advice from academic sources can be very helpful when facing organisational issues and challenges, but its value can be limited unless the advice has real life experience to back it up. For example, would you risk your first bungee jump being harnessed and pushed over a bridge by someone who had read books on bungee jumping, interviewed people who had bungee jumped, analysed the mathematical data, but had never actually done a bungee jump themselves? Me neither.

Another reason that *Loving Leadership* is different is that it doesn't (intentionally) cover the need to be commercial, strategic or global. Don't get me wrong, leadership requires a commercial, strategic and global perspective, that goes without saying, but there are plenty of books, courses, TedTalks, podcasts, etc., for that. This book focuses on the things that are very easy to overlook, easy not to reward because they're thought a bit 'fluffy'/hard to measure, and easy to find reasons not to do. It's the soft stuff. The people-focussed stuff. The emotionally intelligent stuff. The HR stuff.

Ironically, as I will bring to life in this book, ultimate productivity and long-term health of any business is powerfully linked to how every employee *feels* about their manager and leader, which directly relates to what their manager and leader *does* (or doesn't do) to make them feel engaged, motivated and valued. Being commercial, strategic and global has very little bearing on this intrinsic feeling, and therefore limits the offer of any additional incremental effort.

Another key challenge this book invites you to consider is that improvement in the field of 'loving leadership' is about a change in *mindset* much more than focussing on knowledge, experience or process. Why? Because leadership is about *choice*. It's that simple, and that complex. If you are in a genuine leadership role with clearly defined accountabilities, then you have complete autonomy to choose how to spend your time and what you do. With the exception of some mandatory regular meetings (and there really are not many that are completely mandatory), *you* control your time. Yes, you, not all the people who send you meeting invites, email you with their own requests/ demands, call you, text you or even turn up at your desk.

It is very easy to pack your time as a leader with 'stuff'. In fact, it's very easy to drown yourself completely in back-to-back operational matters, crisis management, problem solving, meetings, emails, calls, and the odd working lunch if you can fit it in. Furthermore, many organisations suffer from 'promoting the art of looking busy' and presenteeism, and penalise anyone who looks like they might actually have some time on their hands/capacity.

It is much more difficult to prioritise your time for good, honest, hands-on people leadership when there is so much else to convince yourself rationally needs doing first. This 'hands-on' approach includes (not exhaustively) talking with people about how they are doing, investing time into how to reward and motivate others, thinking about who has done a great job, thanking people, sharing things about yourself with others, getting involved in the social side of things.

To actually choose to do this when there is so much else to do requires a mindset shift, so you have the strength to believe that spending your time on these things does have a better impact on long-term productivity. It requires you to be brave. It requires you to confirm that, yes, you are indeed spending a lot of time talking with colleagues when there is operational chaos going on around you, and profits are down – surely this is a luxury and you clearly don't have a day job, do you. Are you mad? You need to be prepared to face this challenge, and bat it straight back. These choices will have clear and immediate consequences one way or another, which is why leadership is the ultimate risk/reward career choice.

I once worked with a senior executive who was incredulous when I suggested that we should formally build people management/leadership into the regularly monitored performance metrics of – you guessed it – all the company's people managers and leaders. I pushed on with the theme, suggesting that a modest guideline of 20% of a line manager's time should be spent with their team members, and for them to be appropriately recognised and rewarded for doing so.

He suggested that this was an impossible, non-commercial and somewhat naive comment, to which other executives round the table stayed silent and allowed my slow public death to follow. (Note to self: must do a better job of stakeholder management before key meetings!) At the same meeting, he also noted that 'coaching is for wimps' when I tabled the introduction of a global coaching initiative for his leadership team, so this also died. Two deaths in one meeting – not my finest hour of influence! Interestingly, he left this post within a year and left the company soon after. Such is the almost unavoidable direction of travel for leaders who can't adapt to a new model that places people's feelings at the very heart of leadership.

LOVING LEADERSHIP: Introducing the 8 powerful techniques

Exercise: Where are you now?

Before moving into the content of the book, please take two minutes to rate honestly and objectively where you are against all 8 powerful techniques. (Check the contents page for more detailed headings as to what these techniques are referring.)

Score yourself out of 10, where 0 is that you don't ever do it, 10 is that you do it all the time. Just note the scores for now, nothing more:

Give Trust   ....

Care for Others   ....

Be Vulnerable   ....

Shine a Light   ....

Create Magic Moments   ....

Really Listen   ....

Be Sociable   ....

Paint Pictures   ....

We will revisit these scores at the end of the book, and then decide what to do about them.

CHAPTER 1:

GIVE TRUST

'The best way to find out if you can trust somebody is to trust them.'

Ernest Hemingway

Share private Information

Truth be told, you have to give trust to get trust, so the glaringly simple reality is that if you want to have people around you whom you can trust (and what a lovely feeling that is), then you have to ensure that they trust you first. Otherwise the equation will never balance. When people feel that they have been told something private, whether it is confidential, slightly above their pay grade, something that might help them understand other relationships, for example, then they automatically feel more connected to the person who told them.

One of the best leaders I have ever had was brilliant at this. He shared information with me that I found incredibly helpful. It opened my eyes to what was really going on in the organisation. Much of what he shared with me was highly sensitive so he was making a judgment call in giving me his trust, but therein lies the risk/reward conundrum. He took the risk of trusting me to use the information with great care and prudence, and that was exactly what I did.

Because he took the leadership leap of faith to bring me in onto the inside, I repaid that by being loyal and committed to the core. He had my absolute trust. I was prepared to give my all to the relationship and everything I did for him. And by repaying his trust, I became a confidante. He would share more, and I would in effect be coaching him —without realising it, I was harnessing my own skills as an executive coach and trusted advisor that form the bedrock of any good HR director's toolkit.

Once the trust is established, the journey doesn't end there. Unless you are dealing with family or close friends, where trust is usually ingrained, the world of business can be very transactional – so for genuine trust to continue, the cycle of data sharing needs to be topped up, along the lines of:

- I share something privately with you

- You don't share it with others

- You share something privately with me

- I don't share it with others

- Both parties benefit and/or have a stronger relationship as a result

- Result: trust strengthens. The 'Trust Loop' is reinforced

If I miss out any of the steps, or even worse abuse the trust (e.g., it emerges that others know what you shared, or what I shared about you without permission) the trust is broken. It might be possible to mend it once if the relationship is strong, but break it more than once, it will be looking like a habit, and the trust will soon vanish. Your relationship will only ever be transactional, even if you manage yourselves publicly in the same fashion as before. Although others might not notice, both parties will know that deep down the trust has been broken and can't be repaired.

Wayne Mullen, Executive Leadership Director at King agrees:

'Self-disclosure and being vulnerable help in building deeper connections with others. People can then be less cautious themselves. You can loosen them up to be more inclusive, comfortable with diversity of thinking, and risk-taking.'

Be Human

When it comes down to it, there are very few businesses that don't ultimately succeed or fail based on how well people-to-people relationships are fostered. It is a cliché, but it is 'all about the people'. Every business is a people business – suppliers, buyers, sellers, staff, shareholders, customers, strategic partners, consultants, advisers. It's all about people dealing with people.

And we live in a world of reliance on collaboration and crowd sourcing concepts to get things done. So if it is all about people interacting with other people, then you have to ask the question 'What makes the difference in the quality of people-to-people relationships in a corporate environment?' The answer: be *human*. Show your human side.

In an increasingly time-poor, high-pressure working environment, it is very easy just to focus on the task in hand – the business, the strategy, the deal, the contract, the objectives – because your mind is saying 'I really don't have time for small talk, let's crack on and get stuff done'. However, if you need other people to help you make that happen, then you will only get their full commitment to crack on when they really know you, the human you, rather than your 'position power'. The latter will still work, yes, but only to a point.

To get more commitment, try showing a human side *outside* of the actual task – it will go such a long way towards helping people really connect with you. And this is particularly true of leaders whom people want to follow. I can guarantee that if you set yourself the following task and stick to it, the power of your leadership, and relationships with others, will move to a different level entirely:

In every human interaction build in a comment/ observation/question outside of whatever you are doing that gives a glimpse of your personality, interests and viewpoints, likes and dislikes. Regardless of whether others agree or disagree, it creates a connection, makes you interesting, makes you *human*, and makes you someone people will want to follow, work with, engage more deeply with, and find out more about. More importantly, they will give more of *themselves* to you.

Many organisations have seen the benefits of encouraging a human side to their leaders, and it was a successful new concept during my time at Barclays back in the late nineties. The Group HR Director at the time embedded a requirement for all Barclays leaders to 'be human', and wanted HR to lead from the front by putting it into action. It certainly worked. I still recall the image of our One HR Annual Conference, with over 1,000 attendees, being hosted by the Group Training Director dressed in his football referee's kit (with whistle and knobbly knees to boot!) – very un-corporate and completely unexpected, but it worked. It showed a human side.

Whilst this may appear light-hearted, and it did get a few laughs, it actually served the much deeper purpose of breaking down hierarchical barriers, as well as creating a more fun and collaborative event, plus it encouraged many other leaders to have a go. And because of this, although you could see that for some of the other leaders it was very much out of their comfort zone to be so unconventional, everyone really appreciated the efforts and let themselves relax more than normal.

To help bring this further to life, here are some more examples of the technique in action:

- If you are ever presenting to a group of people, always build in a story that says something about you. It could be '*The other day my six-year-old daughter asked me...*' Immediately every person with kids will picture their own children asking them a hard question, and also everyone knows you have kids and something in common.

- Talk about what you do outside of work, e.g. '*Can't wait for the Ryder Cup to start.*'

- If you are late to the meeting, be honest, e.g. '*Traffic was awful*', '*I had a terrible night's sleep last night*', etc.

Take risks on others

One of the inherent flaws of many leaders is not letting go of responsibilities, resources, finances, tasks, projects and even just day-to-day idea creation and problem solving. They want to do it themselves, and in many cases they cannot help themselves. Do you know anyone like this? The micro-management leader? The 'my way or the highway' leader? The 'let me show you the right way' leader? The 'if you want a good job doing, do it yourself' leader? The list goes on...

The problem is often rooted in the usual journey to leadership, because to reach such lofty heights they have probably already got a track record of being successful in terms of *delivery*, *productivity* and *results* as opposed to pure leadership. In many cases, they will have shaped their careers by demonstrating to customers, bosses and organisations that they are consistently better than average, can achieve more than others with faster results and to a higher quality. With this track record, promotions occur, ironically taking them *away* from the very aspects that they were strong at and into the world of management, and ultimately leadership. For example:

- Promoting your best sales account manager to Sales Director

- Promoting your best technical employee to IT Director

- Promoting your best call centre agent to Head of Call Centre

- Promoting your most innovative campaign designer to Head of Marketing

All these are seemingly logical moves within hierarchical structures, but they are often far from perfect. Many such situations can lead to disastrous results where the person fails miserably.

However, do not despair. One of the reasons that these promotions fail is simply this – the newly promoted leader does not take risks on others. Not even tiny risks! They are completely risk averse when it comes to devolving important tasks, accountabilities, and even day-to-day processes. They want to control everything, which in effect means doing everybody else's job for them. They are so familiar with the operational aspects of the jobs they are now leading that they find it impossible to allow others the responsibility to achieve anything without nervously watching to check that they are doing it the right way.

It is helpful to refer to the dictionary definition of 'risk' to illustrate the point: '*Risk – The possibility that something unpleasant or unwelcome will happen*'. And therein lies the real issue. The leader is scared. The control is rooted in ego, reputation, fear. Pretty deep stuff when you think about it.

So how do you let go and take risks on others? It's actually simple: you have to trust. You have to try. And you have to accept that it won't always work out perfectly. Over the years I have found the following three questions particularly powerful when it comes to considering taking risks on others:

- What would be the worst and best outcome?

- How likely is it that the worst will happen?

- What would you do if the worst actually happened?

By following these three questions to a theoretical conclusion, I guarantee that in the vast majority of cases you will realise that the barriers are either all in your mind, or that the benefits outweigh the risks, or that it is not impossible to overcome even if things do go wrong.

Still sceptical? Well, if you need any further convincing that this is the only possible solution, ask yourself, 'How did *I* get my track record?' Exactly – you got it because someone was prepared to take a risk on you. It's time to start giving the same formula a go and let the cycle of success repeat. If you don't, you risk becoming an organisational blocker, and you might find that others soon see you as part of the problem and not the solution.

CASE STUDY: Anna Blackburn, CEO of Beaverbrooks

Beaverbrooks the Jewellers is one of the most successful mid-size companies in the UK, and has been consistently ranked as one of the 'Best Companies to Work' for 12 years in a row, including coming first in 2009. An enormous part of this success has been attributed to its values and leadership ethos, and I talked with the current CEO, Anna Blackburn, about what makes the leadership of Beaverbrooks so effective.

Anna joined Beaverbrooks in 1998 as a sales person having left university seeking a role that fitted with her drivers in life, and she found an immediate connection with their values that was not as forthcoming in other, more corporate, graduate programmes. Over her 17-year career, she moved from the shop floor to ultimately being made CEO in 2013, something that she never thought would have been possible in her wildest dreams when she initially joined.

Anna describes herself as a retailer through and through, and her first ambition was to run her own Beaverbrooks store. She found that her personal style, impact and influence soon led her to positions of more and more responsibility, and that by knowing the business inside out, coupled with her personality, the eventual move to CEO was actually a logical, if not amazing, final step. Furthermore, because the organisation placed great trust in her talents and was prepared to give her the ultimate position of responsibility, this reinforced Anna's belief about placing her trust in others to step up to stretching challenges and inspiring them to deliver great results.

I asked Anna about the other key ingredients of her leadership style that she thinks has driven this success story, and she puts so much of this down to a desire to take plenty of time with people to inspire them; in fact she now aims to spend around 80% of her time with company staff.

One of her first actions as CEO was to commission a staff survey across the business, asking what behaviours *they* wanted from a leader, and she fully embraced the top five responses: honesty, inspiration, competence, care and forward thinking. She then coupled this data with the annual Best Companies survey to form a very rich picture of what was working and what needed developing around leadership.

Anna has a very inclusive style, and is known for running focus groups at the Head Office and stores and then getting things improved and fixed. She has a philosophy that in nearly all people interactions there is a potential win-win to be had and prides herself on a transparent approach and collaborative style. She puts much of her success down to '...investing a disproportionate amount of quality time with key people who can help drive the business forward, and encouraging them to take more responsibility and accountability for making decisions and getting things done'.

A large part of Anna's approach is due to her finding a strong match between her personal values and those of the company. Every employee is part of the 'Beaverbrooks Way', which at its core is all about *'enriching lives and making a positive difference'*. The company values which underpin this purpose are integrity, caring and passion, and they have lasted the test of time with the company since Anna joined all those years ago. In particular, Anna stressed the importance of building deep, long-term relationships with staff and customers, and instilling a climate of trust and responsibility across all 67 stores. Building long-lasting, mutually-beneficial relationships with suppliers is also a key focus for Beaverbrooks who have an outstanding reputation within their trade.

Anna is a role model of living the values and purpose in many ways. She gets heavily involved in activities related to giving back, both by community work and charity work, in line with Beaverbrooks' policy of giving 20% of its post-tax profits to charities every year. She strives to show an accessible and human side, and as a working mum of two, she sets the tone for a flexible workforce that is highly female oriented. Balancing working and home life is encouraged, and led by example in the choices Anna demonstrates herself. All these activities engender a feeling of trust in her as an individual that gives people confidence in her as a caring and genuine leader.

One of the particular leadership behaviours that Anna is not afraid to show is being open to criticism, and the particular example she used was being a role model in inviting direct feedback from others throughout her career. She has always created an environment of trust where people can give her an honest assessment of her strengths and weaknesses, as she explained:

'I sometimes have some pretty hard-hitting feedback. On occasions, on the positive side, people said they really loved my energy, passion and level of animation (which I still have loads of!); however, I was told that people were finding it really hard to meet the standards I set, and never felt anything was good enough. They also said that I didn't spend enough time celebrating successes as we went along, because I was too quick to move to the next thing. As a result, I soon learnt to thank people more, be more aware of the pressure I was creating, and to leave people with more empowerment to achieve things in their own style.'

Anna said that this open invitation is just as relevant now she's CEO as it was 15 years ago. She explains:

'I recently read an article about the 'CEO disease', where in many companies the culture is one where people don't want to tell their CEO bad news, or things that need to be improved either personally or in the business. In many cases, this is driven by either direct or second hand evidence about the CEO's previous emotional and/or angry reactions in other situations which leaves people scared of being the next one in the firing line, so to speak. I never want to come across like that, and hope that everyone will always trust me to embrace honest feedback, and find me authentic, approachable, and true to myself.'

Finally, I was interested to get Anna's view on where leadership goes wrong in terms of things that she has observed over her career. She was quick to explain that, for her, leadership goes wrong when success or results are more about the individual and not the greater good either of the company, society or other people. Her view is that once leadership becomes an intrinsically selfish act, which usually turns into a political agenda for self-gain, then this approach is not sustainable.

Another leadership banana skin she has seen is when leaders have consulted, found out what people want, but then implemented something different and/or what they wanted to do anyway. This is one of the fastest ways to destroy an employee's trust in the company's leadership. Her strong advice to other leaders is, 'If you aren't committed to taking direct action on the answers, then don't ask the question! Or at least spend time explaining why something is not viable'.

Wise words from someone who has clearly shown the benefits of having the courage to ask questions, hear answers, and make powerful relevant changes and improvements accordingly.

EXPERT VIEW: Neville Pritchard, CEO of HR in Flow Ltd

Neville enjoys making a difference to the energy people bring to their workplace and developing organisation performance by harnessing the full potential of leaders, managers and employees. At People in Flow, Neville and his team offer new and unique programmes focusing on trust and enabling energised engagement. At the core of these solutions is the need to build and maintain trust, so he was keen to add some personal reflections to this particular chapter.

'Richard delivers so many helpful insights about trust and the value of trust in this chapter. Stephen

M R Covey highlights the commercial sense behind a high trust organisation: high trust = low costs/low trust = high costs. With the strong business case he made and Richard expounds, why is it not simply the given culture? There are three elements to explore: the individual, the balance between risk and reward and the organisation culture with commercially focused flow. All three impact on whether you will easily give trust.

'Why was Richard so trusted by his line managers throughout his career? Well, having worked with Richard I can confirm that he has always had exceptional commitment, was quick to understand concepts and detail and had a real strength in his understanding of others. There are many dimensions of trust, but one that stands out is that people trust people to do what they know them to be good at, or even exceptional at, – they are committed to it, they enjoy it and are clearly not stressed by it.'

Neville continues: 'People who are very talented are not always trusted to do what they are less proficient at or have less commitment to. These would often be things that they find stressful or just want to keep putting on the "next day" list of activities. So, it is not simply a case of blind trust, it is considered trust you would give. The consideration is appreciated when it's explained when the trust is given and also when not given. This consideration may also unearth greater team efficiencies when considered across your team or organisation.

'The balance of risk and reward is also a factor: how great is the risk of trusting, and how great is the risk of not trusting someone to do what they are very good at? The full implications of assuming the dominant place in all decisions or risk/opportunity moments are many and dangerous. Context and genuine significance is key. Many readers will have seen executive boards operating as operational boards and constraining the potential contributions of expertise by openly showing a lack of trust.

'There is a reluctance to change, a reluctance to shift away from control mode. Risk management is highly important and has to be prominent in the way in which some organisations operate. There are, though, potentially new ways of achieving improved risk management, beyond the current approaches, that change the way in which managers manage and lead. For culture to change, managers have to lead. That leap needs a shift in mindset that embraces difference, value and opportunity. As Richard has succinctly put it: "to be human".

'Often, though, impatience to act in any direction against the advice of experts advising caution or the reverse can destroy the contribution of value and create a negative wiring. The indicators of this include the "everything is urgent" uncoordinated culture – the opposite of the calm leadership that listens, advises, decides and acts with their experts. Giving trust produces positively wired cultures.'

Neville talks about 'The importance of the culture and commercially focused "flow", which is something intangible yet is perceived by many to be an essential lever for improving performance. To be fair, this is a reality. It is the people and the way they interact, collaborate, deliver individual and team value, commit to their performance and behave that generates a collective culture. When aligned, the high trust is more likely. The fewer disconnections to the aspired culture, the more likely intended performance levels will be attained and the higher the internal trust will be, captured in the quote:

'Great minds have purpose, others have wishes.'

Washington Irving

'Excellent service doesn't start with great operations and processes. How many call centre calls have infuriated you with statements such as "It is that way because it is the process!" If process comes before purpose, then in the words of *Dad's Army*'s Frazer, "You're doomed!"

'How well is purpose shared? Daniel Pink, author of *Drive*, states that unless it is an "if this, then that" role, people are motivated by autonomy, mastery and purpose – and in exploring how to influence culture it is the way in which these factors are implemented and sustained that forms the basis of successful change.

'With clear purpose, the alignment of role, action and task is easier. With this established, then trust is easier to achieve with people working in flow. As stated earlier, high trust means low costs (Covey), commercially focused flow is improved and the need for control mode is lessened.

'Thus, as Richard has clearly identified, giving trust is a strength. You may need to create the opportunities.'

Give Trust Summary Checklist: 10 Big Things

1. You have to give trust to get trust – you first!

2. Take calculated risks on sharing private information with others.

3. Show your human side to others, and they will connect with you more.

4. Let go of responsibilities and pass to others, however hard it is.

5. Give people stretching opportunities that they might fail, but at least they will learn.

6. Accept that failure, either by you or others, is an opportunity for growth.

7. Don't break people's trust and think it's OK – it has irreparable consequences.

8. Remember that your way is not the only way – don't prescribe steps to others.

9. You might be wrong. Allow others to challenge you and show alternative paths.

10. Always be honest when things don't go exactly to plan.

CHAPTER 2:

CARE FOR OTHERS

'Too often we underestimate the power of a touch, a smile, a kind word, a listening ear, an honest compliment, or the smallest act of caring, all of which have the potential to turn a life around.'

Leo F. Buscaglia

Treat people like family

To treat people who work with you like family, or as you would your closest friends, is an interesting and challenging concept, but very rewarding. One of the most powerful leadership traits is to ensure that your team, your division, your company, genuinely believes you *care* about them. And people are not stupid, so there is only one way you can ensure people believe this, and that is for it to be true – you can't fake it. And if it is true, it will require a sustained emotional investment from you, which may not come naturally to a lot of leaders.

Imagine yourself in real life, treating people like family members or close friends; stop and think what that would actually look like. You would be interested in them as a whole person. You help them. You involve them. You support them. You protect them. You stand up for them. You think about them. You worry about them – not just between the hours of 9 and 5. It's nice to think that someone feels like that about you, isn't it, rather than thinking, they probably wouldn't ever contact you again if they (or you) left the job. But it's tiring – because people will start trusting you more, the relationships are deeper, and the investment of time to keep the relationship at that level is far more than you would need if you were a purely transactional/analytical leader.

I have met many managers and leaders over the years who, truth be told, couldn't really care less about the people who work for them, or their colleagues, and often their customers too. Work is work, business is business, family is family. It's all black and white. They only really care about results for self-gain, and when people receive rewards for good results they confuse this with thinking the leader rewarding them actually cares about them. Don't be fooled – these types of people don't. You are a cog in a wheel for their self-gain. If your performance drops, they will drop you like a stone and move onto the next person who can help them hit their numbers and targets.

I am not saying this is wrong, and it doesn't make them a bad person, but it does beg the question as to why they are deemed to be an appropriate person to hold a management or leadership position which requires them to inspire others. Maybe for this reason, many people hide the facts about their true (selfish) feelings, only confessing them behind closed doors, or maybe never being honest with anyone about them. Others, meanwhile, feel quite happy to talk openly and loosely about their negative views and selfish outlook, and then wonder what the big problem is and why people won't follow them and do what they say.

Do you know a few people like that? OK, if you think this is a bit harsh, ask yourself this question – how many managers and leaders that you have worked for in the past still actively make the effort to keep in touch with you? They would if they genuinely cared about you, wouldn't they?

And what about people who thank you one minute and rudely bite your head off the next? Inconsistent and erratic behaviour is often an Achilles heel for leaders, because people simply don't know where they stand from one moment to the next – 'Do they like me or hate me?' is a very disconcerting question to have to ask yourself. What do you think leads to sustainable high levels of performance and engagement? How would *you* like to be seen as a leader, including your ethics and motives?

So, flipping things to a positive trait, a really important part of treating people like family is to be *consistent* with your messages and behaviours to those people, both in and out of work. If you genuinely care about them, then you wouldn't be a different person outside work, saying different things that cut across what you purport to be inside work.

Leaders cast a shadow wherever they go, so remember that the minute your consistency drops and your messages get muddied, then people will stop believing in you and you will go down in their estimation.

Here is a case in point: I worked with a leader who impulsively announced his departure from an organisation on a social media page several months in advance. He hadn't agreed any messaging or handover or discussed sensitivities with anyone else, and the announcement had been made on an emotional whim because something hadn't quite gone his way. Many of the people in his department were also 'connections' on the website and read this post cold, with no context or explanation. The team was already unstable, felt undervalued, and the whole purpose of this leader coming into the role had been to knit them back together and make them feel valued with long-term hope. Quite simply, the statement might as well have said, 'You lot won't have a leader in a few months, I have no idea what's happening next, and frankly I don't care because I never really cared about you in the first place' as it would have had the same negative impact.

When the individual was challenged about the major disruption that this public post caused, as well as making other leaders (including his own boss) look incompetent in the process, he replied: 'My social media accounts are not part of the company, and as such this is of no concern to you. I will post anything I choose'. Of course, we live in a free world with freedom of speech, but what do you think? I will leave it up to you decide if you agree or not. My personal advice is to consider your digital footprint through all social media channels seriously, and make sure the words and music match up if you want to be seen as authentic. If you choose to mix work colleagues with social channels then you have created the grey area.

Worry for their wellbeing

...or, to put this section another way, worry about the *whole* person, and every dimension that makes up the profile of a person's general feeling of 'wellness'. Wellbeing means, quite simply, being well in both body and mind. The highest productivity and engagement comes from people who have high levels of personal wellbeing, so don't see this area as just a bit soft. You want your team members to fire on all cylinders, don't you?

Wellbeing has many dimensions, but if you are aware of them, and facilitate an environment that doesn't put them at risk – in fact, ideally, one that enhances a person's wellbeing – it is time very well spent.

Physical health. Advances in technology have improved our lives in many ways, but with the shift to a services sector workforce, with employees now spending an average of 5.4 hours a day at their desk (source: British Psychological

Society), the result is that in the UK we have been fattened up to the point where now 64% of adults are overweight or obese.

There is a direct link between peak physical health and level of productivity, and that goes for office workers as well as athletes. If you and your team are in good shape, take regular exercise, eat sensibly and look after your bodies, a feeling of wellbeing follows. Encourage any opportunity for your team to do something individually or collectively that will promote their physical health. You can even try a 'walking meeting', which is a regular sight in places such as Silicon Valley and New York; make meetings shorter (30 minutes) and reward your team at the end with a coffee or bring in a culture of 'fruit bowls'; promote physical in-company competitions; give discounted staff benefits to join the local gym... all will help the overall productivity.

Conversely, if you and your team don't make the effort to keep physically well, which is already the case with two thirds of the population, I guarantee you will lack the energy, bounce, tempo, confidence, sharpness and influence to work optimally – so lead by example and get yourself in great shape!

Mental health. The most common mental health problem running riot through most workplaces is *stress*. As a leader, I encourage you to be very aware of a) signs of stress, and b) things you are doing that may be causing stress. I must point out that stress is not the same as pressure – in fact, the human body and mind often function better under mild-to-medium pressure than in a laid-back homeostatic state.

If you see regular signs of stress from people around you, take responsibility to help reduce it in any way possible. This is one of the most positive actions a leader can take and will build relationships that are much deeper and more meaningful with those around you. Start by talking to the person showing signs of stress, as they may not even be aware of it themselves.

Usually, any out of character behaviour indicates stress is at play and having a negative impact. This behaviour could manifest as people being over excitable, depressive, short tempered, making mistakes or bad decisions, upsetting people, being over sensitive, talking loudly, not talking at all, drinking excessively, smoking excessively, over-eating, not eating at all, working antisocial hours, a poor sickness record, or even just a change in their general demeanour. Be on the lookout.

Building family life into work. A feeling of wellbeing comes from a genuine belief that when a person really needs to put their family first, they can, and are culturally supported to, do so. As a leader, if you show flexibility with things such as caring for sick relatives, attending school functions, or attending to matters affecting the household (e.g., utility visits), you will find that in the vast majority of cases, the individual will pay you back in spades.

One of the most debilitating things you can do as a leader is make someone feel incredibly bad about doing anything that does not relate to work, and even worse, turning down a reasonable request. If someone misses their child's first sports day or a best friend's wedding, and it was directly because of you, then you can guarantee that you will never get full value back from that person, and will be on your way to losing them.

Sleeping. This is often overlooked, but you really need to make sure that your employees are getting good, regular sleep. Be really conscious about *insisting* they take a break after, for example, a long overnight flight, a few very long nights/early starts, or working at weekends. If you are exchanging emails very late and very early (one of my worst habits that I know I have to change and am working on), then it suggests that your folks are not switching off and getting enough sleep. It's absolutely fine to tell someone that you do not want to see an email from them after 10pm or before 7am unless it is an emergency. You set the boundaries.

Eating and drinking. Set an example. Let people see you eating and drinking sensibly, putting a priority on your own health. Be careful with drinking too much alcohol; again, set an example to others. As Ghandi famously said, 'Be the change that you wish to see…', so you may need to check the mirror first before encouraging people down a path of self-awareness and self-control.

As a caring leader, be aware of people who are drinking or eating to excess/badly and don't be afraid to talk to them about it. However, this is a very sensitive personal area, so you need to be careful and empathetic in how you do this, and perhaps do it as part of a more general 'concern for their health'. They may not have been aware themselves and could well thank you for picking up on something that may not be obvious to them. It's one of those difficult conversations that comes with the territory, otherwise called 'tough love', but you will be respected for not dodging it.

Relaxing and recharging. As a leader, make sure all your staff take their holidays. There is nothing macho about carrying days over year to year. In fact, I recommend that you do not allow any employee to carry over more than five days, so it becomes a 'use it or lose it' benefit. Also, make sure that they take *at least* one block of two weeks every year from their holiday allocation. You will get the benefit far more than if they worked the whole year without a proper break. Taking a long holiday is not only great for recharging, getting things in perspective, and spending time with loved ones, it is also often when some of the greatest moments of insight and inspiration come which can add massive value to the results of the team and the company.

Pursuing hobbies and interests. A job does not define a person. As a leader, you must never forget this. Just because you may be in an artificially created hierarchy where you have more power than others, it does not follow that outside of work things should follow the same hierarchy – people around you probably have talents and interests that they are passionate about, and may be incredibly good at.

A road sweeper isn't a person, it's a job. A factory operator isn't a person, it's a job. It is a choice someone has made because they get something from it, be it money, friendship or purpose. They might be a millionaire. They might do it to fund another business. They might need the money to care for a sick relative and not care what they have to do. It does not mean that they are not capable of more, either within or outside the workplace. It's just a choice. That's all. Be very careful about making assumptions regarding where the talent lies in your company – look carefully!

It is also not for you to judge whether surfing, reading, hiking, croquet, cooking or playing in a band rather than working is an acceptable use of time. Any leader who takes a *'your job should come before everything, barring births, deaths and marriages'* attitude needs to check the calendar – it's the 21st century. Major global shifts have already taken place in attitudes and expectations of working life from Generations Y and Z who see things very differently, and I encourage all readers to keep abreast of these trends if you want to stay sharp.

Talking. *Everybody* needs a sounding board. One of the most powerful skills of a counsellor or psychologist (and a leader) is their ability to listen: to allow the other person to talk in a safe environment and get stuff off their chest. Remember, the act of allowing your staff to talk, to be heard, without necessarily having to do anything about solving the issue can create strong trust and wellbeing in people. If you make time to talk regularly with your staff about work and non-work, it will have a very big positive impact. (This may sound obvious, but so many leaders don't do it.)

Many great leaders have acknowledged the simplicity of talking as a means to build trust and work through issues. As Allan Leighton, the ex-CEO of Asda, points out: 'So much communication I see in businesses involves talking *at* people, in many cases through emails. For me, communication is about talking *with* people, simply having a chat together face-to-face.' More about Allan's leadership philosophy will follow in the 'Really Listen' chapter.

Show them they are valued

This technique costs you nothing other than a bit of regular thought, but 'not feeling valued' is often cited as the biggest reason for a low staff engagement score, and a reason why people ultimately resign from a role. Everybody likes (in fact, needs) to feel valued, but unfortunately many leaders don't do enough to make sure the person really knows this to be true. And this is not just a case of accidentally overlooking it; it is sometimes that the leader is embarrassed to say nice things about someone, or doesn't want to single someone out, or worries that it will create a high expectation of a salary rise and bonus at the next pay round. This is far too over-analytical, because at the end of the day, it doesn't need to be a complicated act. In fact, just two words are often enough to make someone's day – 'thank you'.

There are so many ways that you can show someone that they are valued, but saying thank you is top of the list. It validates that what someone has done did have a purpose for which you are grateful. It validates that they have been spending their time usefully. It validates that they have achieved something. And it validates that they have genuine worth. Very powerful stuff, and so easy to do.

Beyond this simple 'thank you', you have limitless opportunities as a leader to show people they are valued every minute of every day. The more valued people feel, the more engaged they are, the better their commitment and productivity. If you are receptive to seeking out these opportunities, they will jump out at you. In any feedback that you receive where someone has been mentioned and praised, pass it on to that person with a 'great job' or 'well done'. In some cases, it may be that a particular piece of work or output has received praise, but not the person. It is your job as a leader to ensure the people who made it happen get the credit – don't take it yourself. (See section on 'Shine a Light' for more on this.)

From personal experience, I can vouch for the fact that the corporate world is *not* full of cultures where individuals are regularly feeling valued and appreciated – the companies who really get this right are few and far between, and even then, they still rely on managers and leaders to follow through with delivering the recognition. This is a scary thought when you consider the number one reason people leave their job is because of their manager. Funnily enough, I probably felt more appreciated in junior and early management jobs, when perhaps not as much was expected of me so people were more generous with praise. Since then, sadly, only a handful of memorable things stand out that symbolise times where I have genuinely felt valued and appropriately recognised.

One such time was aged 29 when I was nominated onto the Zurich Futures Programme, an intensive 12-month set of highly sought-after experiences for a handful of people chosen for executive potential. I was incredibly motivated, and still draw on some of those experiences today, from having 'personal impact training' with a BBC actress, to the strategy sessions with an esteemed professor at London Business School, to the services of a brilliant personal career coach, such was their quality. I am still grateful to my boss and the company for this true gift.

Another time that stands out was more recently when a global online career development tool – MyCareer@Ogier – was designed and launched over a six-month period to 800 employees across nine jurisdictions. My boss at the time had formed a great HR Leadership Team and we supported each other so much, recognition and thanks was literally flowing between us, and I did feel truly valued. He famously still recalls that we were 'cooking on gas', a phrase that I use, with fond memories attached to it, with my teams when things are going really well.

On the flip side, at many points in my career I have not felt particularly valued or appropriately recognised at all, in some cases completely the opposite, but my own inner drive for results and progression has seen me through. The feeling of having sacrificed so much to get so little, or in some cases to receive criticism and negativity, is a tough pill to swallow. However, never forget that we all have choices, and I have learnt to go with my gut much more these days. Change something or move on when you feel your strengths would be better deployed elsewhere. I have also learnt to gain energy and enjoyment by spending my time actively valuing and recognising others, and gaining fulfilment and joy from *their* progress and successes, perhaps in some way to make up for my shortage of positive experiences in this area over the years.

CASE STUDY: John Diamond, Director at JT Group and Technology Entrepreneur

John is, quite simply, the best leader I have ever had the good fortune to work alongside. He achieves amazing results through the development and empowerment of people, and with an inspirational 'leading by example' style. What sets John aside from his industry peers is that not only does he genuinely care about people, but he spends a large amount of his time ensuring that they are looked after, always putting their needs above his own. He is incredibly modest, self-deprecating, and avoids the limelight like the plague.

In the 2014 UK Best Companies staff engagement survey, John scored a massive 90% on his personal management and leadership score against an organisational average of 65%, the highest across the whole global company of all other line managers. The score was based on the 'Best Companies MC3 (MC Cubed)' tool, which is shorthand for Motivating,

Considering, Caring and Conversing, four of the strongest behaviours that are statistically proven to increase workforce engagement.

In his time as MD of JT's Global Wholesale business, John also presided over the only '3 Star Best Companies' team in the company, the highest possible score for an engaged workforce. (See www.b.co.uk for further background and explanation of the validity and methodology of the tool.) Alongside this, he grew the Global Wholesale business from £7m to £45m revenue in only four years, i.e. over 650% growth. Who says caring isn't commercial or measurable!

So, how does he do it? What's the secret? I asked John to boil it down to the ingredients of his 'secret sauce', and he summarised it as follows: (He apologises for the simplicity of some of it and that it's in Australian, but hopefully makes some sort of sense.)

Provide a safe, happy environment

- Say 'Hello' to everyone on the way in every day. Say 'Thank you' when people leave

- Be close to the team, chat about stuff, listen, share thoughts

- Be flexible on time so they can fit life in, show you trust them, put family before work where possible. Trust will be repaid many times over

- Demonstrate you care; the MD takes responsibility for failure

- Have a few laughs, encourage participation and contribution from all team members

- Celebrate success – always team first, individual second

Try to figure out what people are good at

- Find people's strengths: let them do more of what they're good at, less of what they're not

- Change the role to suit the person, not the person to suit the role – people don't change much in my opinion

- Give them the confidence and space to do their own thing

- Trust them to do well and do the right thing

- Spend time with them, talk about stuff daily

- See each direct report for at least an hour a week individually, as well as the full team

Try to set a good example

- Be calm, reasonable, demonstrate you care about the person

- Do your best to help them succeed

- Spend time talking about what they want, and options for getting there

- Ask questions, listen, say thank you

- Acknowledge good work, identify other areas to think about/improve

- Admit your own weaknesses and development needs to those around you

- Think ahead, plan, try to do the process stuff to keep things moving while others get on and sell

- Be honest and be yourself. Don't try to be something or someone you're not

- Strangely, I think it helps to be a likeable sort of type

Build a team that lives the same values

- Look for the same attitude/value set: those that care and want to do well

- Appreciate others have different skills

- Be flexible on structure, try new things and change

- Be honest about some stuff working, some not

- Maintain diversity – different people with different skills respect and appreciate difference

- Be tolerant – take the good with the bad – accept we're all bad at some stuff. Find other folks to fill the gaps, make sure most time is spent where we're good

- Look out for those that need more structure than others – try to fit to suit

- If someone isn't working as part of the team, exit them

- Be careful about how the team relates. You can feel when the team is working and when it's not. If it's not, jump on it quickly

Although leaders come in all different flavours, I believe that a global movement towards John's style and behaviours would dramatically improve many workplaces. From a personal perspective, I am modelling many improvements to mirror the strengths John has demonstrated.

At the point of writing this book, John had just been entrusted with building a new business division for JT in Asia Pacific and is heading back to his hometown of Melbourne. I have no doubt that John will draw on all his leadership skills and secret sauce to make this expansion a success.

EXPERT VIEW: Alexsis Wintour, Director and Founder of Marbral Advisory Services

Alexsis has been the Executive Director of a highly successful change management consultancy since 2008, and is dedicated to supporting businesses and individuals to realise their potential. Author of *Project Management – Easy as Pie*, tipped as one of the most successful recently published books for people wanting an introduction to managing change, Alexsis also chairs the Chartered Management Institute local branch and sits on the Skills Board for Jersey.

In her view, the single biggest factor in successful change is how leaders take care of their people's wellbeing. Conversely, one of the biggest flaws in change management, and often the root cause of failures, is the *lack* of focus on the people impact, and in particular the lack of attention to the wellbeing of individuals when so much is expected of them. Alexsis has a philosophy that holds all leaders fully accountable for this responsibility, and in her own words shares some of her direct experiences of the benefits of getting the caring part right, as follows:

1. Organisations do not change. People do

'There is no such thing as "organisational change". Change takes place within each person and this happens one person at a time, one step at a time. It is people's collective momentum that moves an organisation forward. Do not overlook this and be blinded by project plans and traffic light reporting against milestones. These will not bring about the changes that you wish to see, and may cloud your vision.

'Too many times I have seen organisations create a formulaic approach to deal with change, be it brought about to beat the rising competition, deal with regulatory challenges, or develop new products. It's often paired with a mission statement, a two-day, 'off-site', new organisational design, and some links to performance. This has little to no chance of working. It has failed to build in the people elements of any change effort.

'Richard wisely observes that the major change programmes that he has worked on were successful because of the collective efforts and attitudes of the team around him, and remarked, "Recognition and thanks was literally 'flowing' between us." This is about transformational leadership and it couldn't have been experienced if the team suspected that the leaders were being anything less than authentic in why they wanted the change and how important each individual was to them. Consequently the changes that Richard led had a significant impact on each person, and as a result the value of the company. Starting with the people was the right place to begin. Most organisations and leaders miss this.'

2. Winning people's hearts and minds to engage in the change requires great, authentic leadership

'How often have you seen waves of corporate change programmes rolling across the landscape resulting in little impact and huge cost? Why don't they work?

'I would argue that change takes place where the rubber hits the road as I have seen the most change when the direct line manager leads it. This is because people relate to their direct report – that's where they feel most understood. Their direct leader cares how they feel, can articulate what's in it for them, and can offer direct support and guidance that is relevant to their daily work.

'As Richard points out, people know when they are a "cog in a wheel for their [leaders'] self-gain", they know when leaders are relentlessly pushing down from the top for results which mean more to them than to the individuals they are affecting. Take his advice and worry about the *whole* person, as this is without a doubt the secret to unlocking significant potential.'

3. Change causes stress and the natural reaction is resistance

'Change leaders take care of people through every step of the process. Orchestrating a complex change process throughout the organisation is the responsibility of the leadership. This happens in a series of stages, and includes ambition, holding people to account, recognising those that have made progress, giving people the skills and resources, and knowing where to start to create early success, i.e. articulating the "what's in it for me?".

'This means significant investment. This means recognising that change is constant. This means that it cannot be taken lightly. Leaders need to be ready to support their people through each stage, and these stages happen in a sequence. Leaders need to expect performance to drop as the change moves through denial, anger, negotiation to acceptance. I have often used the "valley of despair" diagram to show this, and people can mark on it where they are (opposite).

Once you've asked a few questions, you will be able to predict where your organisation is on the change curve. There are lots of techniques, models, tools and experienced individuals who can help speed you through the valley, but all of them will come back to the same observation – that *people* make change happen, and caring for them and their wellbeing is essential for success.

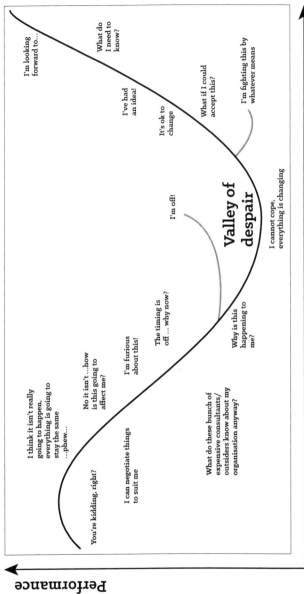

Time

Performance

You're kidding, right?

I think it isn't really going to happen, everything is going to stay the same ...phew...

I can negotiate things to suit me

No it isn't ...how is this going to affect me?

I'm furious about this!

What do these bunch of expensive consultants/ outsiders know about my organisation anyway?

The timing is off ... why now?

Why is this happening to me?

I'm off!

I cannot cope, everything is changing

Valley of despair

I've had an idea!

It's ok to change

What if I could accept this?

I'm looking forward to....

What do I need to know?

I'm fighting this by whatever means

Care for Others Summary Checklist: 10 Big Things

1. Allow yourself the emotional space to care for people, and genuinely show it.

2. Create time to worry about everyone's wellbeing, physical and emotional.

3. Give a warm welcome to people when they arrive, and thank them when they leave.

4. Stay vigilant to signs of stress being shown by others, and act to help reduce it.

5. A job title does not define or pigeonhole a person – don't underestimate anyone.

6. Take ultimate responsibility for failures – protect others from politics and reprimands.

7. Regularly talk with people about work and non-work issues and priorities – listen hard.

8. Support people to put important family and personal commitments ahead of work.

9. Actively ensure your staff take all their holidays, including 2+ weeks in one block.

10. Actively seek opportunities to say thank you and well done to others regularly.

CHAPTER 3:

BE VULNERABLE

'Vulnerability sounds like truth and feels like courage.
Truth and courage aren't always comfortable, but
they're never weakness.'

Brené Brown

Admit when you are wrong

Brené Brown, an expert on social relationships, conducted thousands of interviews to discover what lies at the root of social connection. A thorough analysis of the data revealed what it was: *vulnerability*. Vulnerability in this context does *not* mean being weak or submissive. To the contrary, it implies having the courage to be yourself. It means replacing professional distance and cool with uncertainty, risk, and emotional exposure, good examples of this being the courage to admit when you got it wrong, and knowing when and how to apologise.

Although saying 'It was my fault' or 'Sorry' might sound simple to do, these small words can be extremely hard for many leaders to say directly. There are a lot of reasons for this, all of which can stop this step happening:

- Childhood conditioning that getting things wrong is bad

- Worried for your job if your boss thinks you are unreliable

- Worried it will affect you financially (e.g., performance bonus)

- Saving face: don't want to be judged or criticised

- Concerned that others will not hold you in high regard

- Ego gets in the way, thinking that you are always right

The truth is, we all make mistakes, nobody is perfect. And although this is a well-worn cliché, you really do learn from your mistakes – the biggest character-building experiences in life and work often come from not getting things right (sometimes getting them badly wrong) and improving as a result by doing things differently next time round.

Some of the best and most highly regarded leaders I have either worked with or observed have, typically, been good at this. They have had the self-confidence to admit when they have got something wrong, or even to say that they have *really* screwed something up. Ironically, it often makes them a stronger leader because others then think:

- Well, if he/she can make a mistake, then I can, and it's OK

- Maybe there are things I can help this leader with

- I should have the courage to make decisions and not worry if the odd one doesn't work

- He/she must be a very honest person with high integrity, not a political manipulator

- I would like to work for/follow that person. He/she creates a climate I would be happy in

Making an apology is one thing, but *how* you make it, and what you say, is equally important. Politicians are famous for 'sort of' apologising, but in a very long-winded way, heavily caveated with explanations, and often avoiding the word sorry. The opposite approach is far more powerful – 1. say sorry, 2. don't add anything to make excuses, and 3. do it quickly and succinctly.

Furthermore, getting your apology in first can be very disarming if someone was going to get emotional about the mistake, or had planned to expose you and your apparent failings, perhaps in an effort to paper over their own shortcomings. It's hard to argue with someone who is saying 'I was wrong, my mistake, you were right'. Try it – the disagreement doesn't last long (and you also get to stay in control)!

Be honest when you don't know

On this point, I speak mainly from observation rather than being a shining role model, as I am historically flawed at saying 'I don't know'. I have worked on this shortcoming over the years and have found internal tools that kick in to help me pause and reflect, rather than try and answer. Although I am mainly 'cured' in the work environment, I still slip back into old habits at home. Ask my wife – when I say 'I know xyz' it actually means 'it's *possible* I know xyz'. I love to answer a question. I see it as a challenge. And I am competitive, so it's great to be right. But truth be told, this is not a good trait, and not good leadership – so I must do better in this regard.

The reality is, I believe that so many of us are conditioned from early school onwards to give an answer. As a child, saying 'I don't know' could lead to people thinking you are not clever. A bit dim. It risks being embarrassed. What if everyone else knows, but you don't? How stupid might you feel?

And on the flip side, getting an answer correct, and quickly, would gain you praise and rewards. So the game was always to get in fast and hope it was broadly correct.

No time for reflection.

Conversely, saying 'I don't know' as an adult is actually an incredible strength. It shows inner confidence in differentiating between fact and fiction, truth and half-truths, and drives your integrity stock skywards. In many cases, if you say you don't know, there is a queue of people around you who feel invited in to help you. Impress you. Inform you. Provide the answer for you. It's amazing, but it has quite the opposite effect than your worst childhood fears would have you believe, so give it a go.

Richard MacKinnon, Insights Director at the Future Work Centre, believes that accepting that others might have better and more fact-based answers than you is a powerful step for a leader to take, although very difficult psychologically for many. As Richard explains:

'A key challenge for leaders is to remain open to new ideas and ways of doing things, especially when they've championed something else in the past. It can be tempting to cling on to methods, processes and attitudes because "We've always done it that way", or "It's best practice", or "It was my idea in the first place". Contemporary leaders should really be focused on the evidence behind the advice they receive or indeed give to others. Is it gut feel? Habit? Perceived wisdom? Might it be a fad?

'Understanding what works in your organisation, and why, requires a more objective approach, using evidence and data from a range of sources, a range of voices. And if the evidence suggests a different course of action, leaders should be open to changing their mind and adopting new approaches and mindsets. It can be uncomfortable, but it's critical if progress is to be made.

'Brave leaders seek out evidence and ask questions about why things do or don't work and navigate the business accordingly. They also role model evidence-based decision-making for their colleagues and demonstrate that changing course is not a sign of weakness, rather a positive adaptation to new information.'

However, this personal improvement is only a part of the solution to create a climate where vulnerability is accepted. Leaders have a wider role to play in this shift, as one of the major cultural issues in many companies is that there is not a climate where saying 'I don't know' is accepted and encouraged. It's great if, as a leader, you learn to say 'I don't know', but you still have a key role to practise what you preach, which means you need to embrace rather than penalise when others do it. Do your pay and reward systems support calling out mistakes, or do they promote 'Keep your head down and cover your back'? How do you react when you need something and someone says 'I don't know'? I have worked for many leaders, and let's just say they've covered the whole spectrum of responses.

Jon Bacon, co-founder of Speak the Speech, shared his personal journey of acceptance that not being right, or first, or best at everything, or knowing everything, is not such a bad thing after all:

'When I was a kid I *had* to be first. I was the oldest of four brothers and they were my competition. And maybe because I was the oldest, I had to be first. First to eat my dinner. First to answer Mum's question. First to get to the car so I could grab the best seat. First in running races. Always first. I also had to be the best. Best behaved so I would win the £5 prize we got on holiday for the Best

Behaved Boy. Best at exams. Best at playing football, cricket, rugby. Always the best. I must have been such a pain in the arse. In fact I know I was a pain in the arse because my wonderful brothers are quite happy to remind me that I was a pain in the arse now that we are all in our 40s!

'This competitive spirit may have served me well as an adult on occasions. It gave me a drive and a will to succeed. I became an actor and I strove to be the best actor. I wasn't doing too badly either until it was pointed out to me at drama school that I lacked any vulnerability. Vulnerability? I thought. What do you mean vulnerability? I couldn't even grasp the concept, let alone *show* any. Inherently, everything in me screamed, "Be a winner! Don't show any weakness! You *have* to be first!"

'Unsurprisingly my acting career floundered...

'Nowadays my work allows me to meet new people every single day at all levels. Without a shadow of a doubt the best people I have worked with have been the ones who show humility, modesty and vulnerability. Interestingly they are not always the leaders, though I suspect they soon will be. They may not know this, but I am sure I have learned far more from them than they will have learned from me. And the biggest thing I learned from them is that you don't have to lose your drive or passion to be vulnerable. It is not a case of swapping one thing for another.

'Dan is a leader I help to write and perform speeches. He has an incredible drive and, at times, an almost childlike passion for new ideas and creativity. And he lays himself bare. Totally. He is happy to talk about successes, but equally he is happy to talk about his failures, his flaws and his shortcomings. "I need you Jon. I'm not clever enough to structure this paragraph so that it delivers what I want it to." Dan is hugely intelligent, just not at everything.

'Just before I meet him I always worry. Can I *really* help this guy today? He is brilliant at what he does. Does he know I am basically just a failed actor? But my worries are always dispelled within ten minutes as he asks me all about *my* family, *my* work. He asks me how my youngest got on at that football match he was going to play which I'd briefly mentioned the last time we met three months ago. In fact, he is fascinated by everyone he talks to, and not surprisingly his 1,500 staff love him and repay this genuine interest by plugging every gap, hole or shortcoming to protect him.

'Discovering what vulnerability means has been the single biggest influence on my career and the progress of my company. I surround myself with people who are much cleverer than me and who can help me answer those "I don't know" questions. I am still competitive, but luckily I am not good enough at anything these days to always win, so I have had to learn how to lose!'

Don't take yourself too seriously

From a personal angle, I really was a late starter regarding any real understanding of the power, influence and respect that can be derived from self-deprecation. The concept of it actually being a strength to put yourself down, make fun of yourself, make jokes about how bad you are at stuff, talk about things you have screwed up, pick apart your personality flaws, was inherently at odds to my own (early) map of life.

And I know that I am not alone. As Jon Bacon just candidly shared, so many of us are conditioned through life with mantras such as be strong, be a winner, don't show your weaknesses, cover the cracks, be perfect, always deliver, don't mess up, grin and bear it, gloss over your mistakes, don't trust others, look after number one, be the best, be a role model, etc. And it is draining, isn't it!

Oddly, as a leader the reverse approach is often true in terms of how you can win friends, followers, and actually be seen as a higher performer and stronger leader to those around who are forever striving (and often failing) to impress and be brilliant. Assuming that the leader in question is not actually incompetent, and that they do have a track record of being a good leader in certain aspects, then building a regular dose of self-deprecation goes a long way to securing deeper levels of engagement from those around you.

To look at parallels in other fields of work, some of the most successful comedians in the world are incredibly self-deprecating, and look at how successful they are, how much the audience warms to them and bonds emotionally to their material.

A recent academic study confirms that leaders who adopt a style of humour involving laughing at themselves, but not their colleagues, are seen as more likable, trustworthy, and caring. The researchers hypothesised that, regardless of whether people actually thought a leader was funny, self-deprecating jokes would be seen as an expression of a leader's values and concern for others.

'We chose humour as a mechanism through which leaders express their concern for others (vs. themselves) because of the potential for humour to be both a weapon to harm others and a tool to build relationships,' say researchers in the *2013 Leadership & Organisation Development Journal.*

The study concluded that leaders who focus on the wellbeing of others, a style known as 'transformational leadership', are more likely to earn the trust and goodwill of their employees. Poking fun at themselves is one of the ways in which leaders can de-emphasise differences in status between themselves and their employees, providing evidence of their concern for others.

To look at it another way, it is about being a humble and modest person. By putting yourself down, or simply being open and honest about your weaknesses and areas for development, you are bridging the gap with people around you, whether hierarchical, social or technical. It makes you a more human person, not a robot, and someone that others can relate to. It also gives people permission not to be perfect, and to be less concerned about taking a few calculated risks or trying something new without fear of failure. In fact, it's hard to find a genuine downside to this approach, other than perhaps overplaying the characteristic, which might seem less authentic.

So ultimately, regular acts of self-deprecation from leaders actually drive a non-hierarchical culture of innovation and collaboration. Who would have thought it? Try it for yourself, and see what response you get. You may be (pleasantly) surprised with the results...

CASE STUDY: Lynne Weedall, Group HR Director at Dixons Carphone

Dixons Carphone plc is Europe's largest consumer electronics and telecoms retailer, operating in over nine markets, 2,500 stores, and with 40,000 staff, and at the time of writing had just reported annual profits that are up 24% on last year in a market that has been very tough and volatile over recent years. Lynne Weedall has led on all aspects of the People Agenda across the group following the merger of Dixons and Carphone in August 2014, prior to which she was the group HR Director for Carphone Warehouse and was also responsible for group strategy and communications.

Lynne has a clear philosophy on what makes a great leader, which at its core is about being authentic and genuine, and ensuring that there is no dissonance between what you say and what you do. She believes that the hallmark of being true to yourself, living by your own values and beliefs, is essential for people to believe in you. Therefore, leaders need the courage to be who they are, rather than perhaps what they think others want them to be. This requires a level of vulnerability as it does leave you open to criticism, but at least people can choose whether to follow you or not.

Another leadership trait that Lynne feels is key is curiosity, as it unlocks so many other pieces of information that help drive relationships and companies forward. With curiosity comes questioning, and then with good listening skills you can get a range of views and answers that help you address things from different angles and viewpoints, which is the root of thinking differently. Other elements that she also holds in high regard are drive, passion and resilience, which she sees as very underestimated being as they are skills whereby leaders can recharge, regroup and reenergise.

In terms of her own success, she puts a large part of it down to assembling a great team around her, and never compromising on the quality and diversity of people that she hires. Then she spends time valuing and nurturing them in order for them to deliver great work that helps the team succeed. She also prides herself on having straightforward conversations, and focussing on the things that matter, keeping things in perspective with a pragmatic level head. With this, she is also a lady of great drive and courage, which helps her face whatever is in front of her.

But above all, Lynne sees a large part of her ultimate success as being able to show vulnerability along the way, even when it has been incredibly tough to do so. By her own admittance, she has made a few howlers in her career, which have ended up being the key defining moments that have shaped her and helped her improve as a leader.

One of these moments was fairly recent for Lynne, regarding the Dixons Carphone merger that she managed the People Agenda for, as she explains:

'I completely underestimated the level of emotion in the system, and how hard it was for everyone on both sides of the transaction. From a personal point of view, I was finding it just as hard, and I liken it to being a trapeze artist in that I had to let go of one bar to travel successfully to the next, and this was hard for everyone. The level of regret and loss was far greater than I had planned for, which I have admitted and accepted.'

Another example that Lynne remembers clearly is when she had a career move from Tesco to PetSmart, now known as Pets at Home. Her approach was to take all the fantastic learning frameworks and philosophies from Tesco, which had been all about staff empowerment, and apply them to PetSmart. She soon found out that what the new organisation was crying out for was some good, old-fashioned operational control, and as Lynne says:

'I couldn't have got it more wrong, and learnt there and then never to assume that you know the answer if you are in a new environment'.

However, Lynne had the courage and confidence to be honest about this. She became the leader she is today by being comfortable with admitting when she got it wrong.

Lynne also recounts her time seeing Sir Charles Dunstone, the founder of Carphone Warehouse, in action, and puts a great deal of her own leadership success down to what she has learnt from him. In particular, Charles always encouraged his management team, and all staff, to keep things in perspective. He is famous for saying, 'We are not saving lives here, we sell phones and TVs', so he was very matter of fact and modest about the reality of the business.

Furthermore he often talked about how lucky he was, rather than taking credit or seeking fame. He even explained how many of his ultimate successes arose out of taking risks and facing up to mistakes, pointing to the launch of free broadband by Carphone Warehouse. Everyone was completely unprepared for the popularity of this deal and couldn't meet the demand. This resulted in many complaints and nearly brought the business to its knees as it struggled to cope with how over-subscribed it was. However, from the embers of this reckless (on reflection) decision, a new and highly successful FTSE100 Business – Talk Talk – was subsequently born.

There is another example that for Lynne demonstrated Charles' genuine humility and vulnerability in terms of being open about mistakes and being selfless in an effort to help others who might be going through the same pain. A well-documented corporate failure was the cursed opening of Heathrow's Terminal 5, which soon became a laughing stock and resulted in an aggressive counter-marketing campaign by Virgin which wrestled away hundreds of high-value customers and millions of pounds with it. At its worst point of PR coverage, Charles phoned the CEO of Terminal 5 to offer any help, support and advice he could give, on the basis that 'I have been there myself'. This really was a class act from an authentic and humble leader.

Finally, I asked Lynne whether there are areas of leadership that, from her experience, don't work anymore, or don't help foster the right climate. For her, it is any leaders who simply take *themselves* too seriously – just because the work is taken seriously, it doesn't mean that the time for play, fun, humour and laughing is moved away from the workplace. Lynne believes leaders who are too serious will struggle to adapt to the future models of driving corporate success through people. In addition, Lynne avoids working with or for anyone who lacks courage or boldness and is too afraid to make a decision. She believes all leaders should take responsibility for difficult decisions rather than procrastinating or hiding behind others – a strong trait that she certainly lives by herself!

EXPERT VIEW: Dale Ibbotson MBE, Chairman of 3D Group

Linked to facing up to mistakes is the ability to share openly with others when things are going wrong, and this requires a level of humility and authenticity that separates OK leaders from great leaders. Dale Ibbotson MBE is the Chairman of 3D Performance, a global strategic leadership consultancy, and getting leaders to face up to the reality of their current situation is usually the first and most important step that Dale gets on the table at the start of any assignment. I can vouch for this first hand, having partnered with him on two challenging assignments at different organisations, and Dale brings to life the need for vulnerability driving collaboration in his own words as follows:

'3D Performance specialises in advanced leadership and teamwork. People quite understandably challenge me on what exactly that means.

'Let's quickly go back to the DNA of 3D. Many years ago I worked in the field of Long Range

Reconnaissance, developing teams that could disperse around the world and yet maintain incredibly high standards of communication and focus. Exactly the attributes that a modern team needs in this day and age of a global market and remote leadership. We also work very closely with the fast jet and test pilot community with whom we share many disciplines and cultures. Currently we recruit, develop and deploy teams on a global basis for the benefit of multinational companies.

'The commonality both those elite cultures have is that they rely upon a spirit of true collaboration based on the principles of complete honesty and openness at all times as to how people are performing. There are no hidden agendas – they are strictly forbidden. There is no veiled speech; what needs to be said is said clearly, constructively and to the point. Challenges are always objective, mission-centric, and never personal.

'The modern business environment actually makes it very difficult to create a truly collaborative culture. There is a constant fear of being seen to make mistakes, to show weakness, to display uncertainty. The more senior the position, the more exposed the individual feels, and consequently the more protective and restrictive they are in terms of behaviour and their willingness to share all the information they have.

'We spend more time now de-risking, desperately trying to avoid perceived hazards, many of which when assessed rigorously are hardly of note, when we could all be sustaining pace and momentum within our highly competitive and rapidly changing markets. Actively learning through doing, debriefing en-route, ensuring we are continuously driving towards our objectives. A dynamic versus set-piece approach.

'To give an example, I was working to assemble an executive leadership team (ELT) in America, and it had been stated very clearly as we pulled this team together that there was going to be a culture of complete openness. Any problem that was openly raised would never attract criticism if presented in complete honesty from the outset. Once done, it then became the responsibility of all members of the ELT to support the individual concerned collectively to drive the best solution.

'One team member was clearly uncomfortable with this concept. During a break, he took me to one side and said, "You have to understand that I come from an environment where if you admitted things like this within the board you would be taken to the cleaners".

'I said, "I can simplify your dilemma: if you are not completely honest and collaborative, and if anyone of us finds out that you have withheld information, your career within this team is over. Being completely authentic and honest is now a core drill and there is no negotiation on standards at this level of leadership. Make a choice."

'Once back in the boardroom, it was clear he was deeply uncomfortable with the concept. However, when it came to his turn to brief the ELT on progress, he said, "I feel I am taking an incredible risk here, but

I am going to trust the integrity of the people around me. The IT project my team is responsible for is actually eight weeks behind schedule in my personal view, not the three weeks they are claiming, and I am deeply concerned that we are looking at a $500K overspend on budget. I have several options which I think we can potentially use to try and salvage the situation, but being completely honest, none of them fills me with confidence, least of all the one they want to run with. So if we are really going to work like this, I am completely open to any input or ideas."

'It has to be said this was a moment of truth for the entire team as you could have heard a pin drop after that statement. Dropping $500K in their environment previous to this day would have resulted in some rapid restructuring. The first step was taken when another team member started by saying, "Let's scrap the agenda and focus on this for the next two hours. Give us the details and we'll see what we can all do."

'One hour later, there was a robust operational plan which had reduced the cost to $200K. Despite the best efforts from the considerable expertise around the table, nothing could be done about the delay, but by now everyone affected had planned in advance so that they could act accordingly and minimise the impact and disruption.

'I was rightly challenged by the Chairman when debriefing. However, when I pointed out the different outcomes between the two scenarios, he fully embraced the spirit of open collaboration, and to give him full credit, drives it now from the heart. In addition, I pointed out that it was the previous culture that had created the problem in the first place. Due to the pressure of conflicting organisational priorities, the regional IT role had become isolated. The whole point of having a mutually supportive leadership team had been lost.

'The ELT team two years on from writing this note is truly exceptional and still genuinely collaborative – I will leave it to you to work out what would have happened if we had let this play out within a traditional risk averse leadership model.

'To create a true spirit of collaboration requires genuine leadership as it will not always be pretty, and you are going to have to react, support or deal with people accordingly. It requires you to be ruthless in recruitment and the maintenance of standards. However, the standards are not complex: open, honest, authentic people who are selfless with those around them and collaborate naturally. That, once established, is the very foundation of some of the best leadership teams it has been my privilege to work with.'

Be Vulnerable Summary Checklist: 10 Big Things

1. If you are sorry, then use the word sorry – don't politically skirt around an apology.

2. Think about your mistakes and commit to doing things differently in the future.

3. When something has gone wrong, get your apology in first, before someone demands it.

4. Regularly take opportunities to make fun of yourself and your character flaws.

5. Showing you are not perfect drives innovation in others and the courage to take risks.

6. If you don't know, then don't make it up – say 'I don't know' – harder than it seems.

7. But...don't forget to follow up when you don't know – make it your business to know!

8. Never publicly penalise people around you who say they don't know something.

9. Being clear when you don't know can invite a positive wave of contribution from others.

10. Build reward and recognition systems that value a trying-failing-learning-try again loop.

CHAPTER 4:

SHINE A LIGHT

'There is more hunger for love and appreciation in this world than bread.'

Mother Teresa

Give public recognition

Don't get confused by the words here – when I say public recognition I don't mean embarrass someone publicly by pointing them out in front of others in a face-to-face environment, making them go bright red in the process. Yes, this might be appropriate in some circumstances, but it is also some people's worst nightmare, so be aware of the person's feelings.

My definition of giving public recognition is '*to make other people, who might otherwise not have known, aware of a particularly good job or deed that someone has done, and the value they add*'.

With this interpretation, there are hundreds of ways you can do this as a leader. Also, just because you are the leader, don't limit yourself to giving recognition south into your direct line reports. Great leaders call out great efforts north, south, east and west. It doesn't matter if they are your peers, reports, suppliers, boss, stakeholders, customers, etc., it is the act and habit of calling out a good effort that will win people's respect and improve your value and trust with them.

By far the simplest, and lowest risk, is an email. I would encourage you to never sit on information where someone is shown to have helped in a stand-out way and not pass it on in some shape or form. For many people, there is nothing more motivational than a simple well done via emails written by more senior people, copying in other influential people – this takes literally 10 seconds and has such a disproportionate impact. Perhaps even copy in the executive board, thereby getting the well done endorsed and making sure the person feels really valued. This needs to be both habitual and proactive – you need your radar set to 'look for reasons to say thank you and well done'.

Another important aspect of recognition, which is a form of feedback, is the timeliness of it – the closer your acknowledgment of a good act or contribution is to the act itself, the more powerful and authentic the message, and the higher the chance of embedding repeatability of that behaviour in the individual. They will feel compelled to do more of the same, maybe better.

As a leader, there are going to be times that you will either choose or be required to do a recognition presentation or speech to somebody – high responsibility indeed. There won't be many times in someone's life that they experience such a formal event. It might be an award, retirement, successful project – whatever – where etiquette and common sense tells you that a proper public thank you is needed. In these situations, I have one piece of advice: prepare.

Make sure you know the details behind the recognition. The people involved. The times it happened. The challenges faced. The outcome. Then you will come across as authentic. There is nothing worse than a leader going through the motions of giving recognition when they really don't know why they are doing it – in fact, it can make people feel less valued, so beware!

Be a talent spotter

Taking time and energy to spot talent is one of the responsibilities most overlooked by many leaders in that they just don't acknowledge the importance of securing the next generation of the company. I believe that this is mainly the product of three recent phenomena that have converged to create an unsurprising mindset for some leaders:

- No more jobs for life for leaders, far more risk, shorter tenure, shorter reward cycles

- Much more job hopping by Generation Y and Z so no guarantee that they will stay

- Stress and time-poor leaders not spending enough time engaging with their own employees

The problem is for many leaders, although they would never admit it publicly, that their cost/benefit analysis concludes 'Why bother spending time being a talent spotter' as a) it might be my successor that benefits, not me, and b) the person might not hang around anyway?' This leads to an inevitable, and ultimately flawed, recruitment strategy, namely to default to hiring externally and overpaying for 'finished article candidates' who can deliver faster for the leaders' personal benefit. This quick fix is also often demotivating for talented internal people who feel overlooked.

However, this is not a sustainable culture both in terms of cost and philosophy. More accurately, it's lazy leadership, ultimately wasting the company's (and shareholders') money, and indicating that you wouldn't spend the time to think about the longer-term implications of your decision. So the next time you are involved in a debate to hire someone fast, expensive and external, take a while to reflect on how this could be avoided, and what the unintended consequences might be.

Leadership and management theory has evolved greatly in the last 20 years, but the identification and fostering of talent still remains one of the most powerful, impactful and selfless things that a great leader can do. It is your role as a leader to 'reinvent the football team' every few years – you cannot possibly expect to keep trying to put the same players on the pitch week after week, year after year, and keep winning. Your squad will pick up injuries, run out of ideas, and some players will jump to other clubs.

So you have to offset this risk – constantly mix it up with a blended diversity of ages, gender and culture, the strong with the agile, the creative with the tactical, the spontaneous with the conservative, the fresh eyes with the wise owls. That's what makes winning teams. In this regard, a high level of fluidity and forward planning is also required, in that you need to ensure you can call on the right people to deliver in the right place at the right time, and in a way that is in alignment with your vision and priorities.

And finally, don't just be a talent *spotter* (reactive to opportunities). Be a talent *seeker* (proactive to create the chances to unearth the next generation of talent). The best talent isn't just going to fall at your feet. You may get lucky every now and then with a good candidate for a job, or a referral from your trusted network, but in many cases you may be beaten to the post. To have a pipeline of real, long-term, viable talent, you need to be seeking them in everything you do, both within your organisation and also externally/globally, as follows:

Internally: how involved do you get in coaching and mentoring talented folks? How visible are you at learning and development events? How much getting-back-to-the-floor work do you do? How active are you on blogs and internal communications?

Externally: from events, to customers, to LinkedIn, Facebook, Twitter, YouTube, Professional Body Publications, lists of degree qualifications and prize winners, Young Business Awards, committees, lobby groups – the list is endless.

Sounds easy, I know, but you need to care enough to make the effort to look, engage, and ultimately employ those precious unpolished diamonds of the future.

Let others lead

This might sound like a paradox, but one of the most empowering traits that a leader can have is to let *others* do the leading. The skill and intuition to match priorities with people and allow them complete autonomy to make a difference is a rare quality indeed – but it's a little more sophisticated than just the empowerment part. There is an even more important part to play, from this point through to the successful delivery of what was required, which is to be there for your people without them really realising. This can include (not exhaustively):

- Managing key stakeholders who might be a thorn to successful delivery

- Ensuring that the appropriate tools, finances and resources are made available

- Informally coach and/or mentor with passing chats, a cup of tea, etc.

- Acknowledge early wins and small milestones to boost their confidence

Letting others lead has many benefits, not least giving yourself more time to look at the bigger picture, prepare for the future by following market trends, build new relationships, walk round the business – all the 'I must do's' that you just don't get round to doing when you are bogged down with operational leadership. From the viewpoint of the empowered person, they feel trusted, motivated, perhaps healthily scared. It pushes them and energises them, and engagement flies off the scale.

But there's one caveat: take care to give the *right* opportunities to the *right* people. That's what will differentiate you as a great leader. The concept of letting others lead is only half the issue; it's all about your judgment, intuition and forensic analysis that matches people with opportunities.

Speaking from personal experience, this type of stretch opportunity was given to me by an inspirational HR Director when I was aged 29 and worked for Zurich UK as an HR consultant. The Zurich UK Life Insurance Business was in the process of being sold for $500m, which included the outsourcing of several departments by way of TUPE transfer. This deal had enormous implications for every aspect of people-related issues, and needed an HR Lead to sit on the project board to ensure that the deal went through and all people aspects were owned and managed.

Although this would have been in the sweet spot for my line manager's HR experience, he gave me the opportunity in its entirety, maintaining an executive sponsor role when I needed him. I worked on the Project Board alongside the very best technical and operational leads in the company who represented IT, finance, operations, claims, customer services and PR, and in a 12-month microcosm learnt an enormous amount about every aspect of merger and acquisition challenges as we supported each other across all these functions.

My boss acted as a coach and sounding board as I faced one challenge after the other, but ultimately he made me feel empowered to drive through a range of HR interventions with his full backing. It is probably the most engaged I have ever felt on a piece of work, and for 12 months it never crossed my mind what time of day or night it was, what I was getting paid, or where it might lead. I had a simple, big, clear objective which gave me a laser focus and motivation off the scale.

The project concluded and was a resounding success. The deal had gone through, and the affected workforce had been successfully transitioned across to Swiss Re and CSC, culminating in one of my most memorable career highlights on the top floor of the Gherkin in London with a live jazz band and several hundred people who'd been involved in the project. The opportunity arguably set up my ability to secure my first HR Director role soon after, for which I am forever in debt to my boss at that time. For this reason I am always looking to do the same for my team members to this day. In fact, at the time of writing, JT are in talks regarding a merger with Airtel, a fantastic HR project which I have empowered my Head of Organisational Performance to lead –despite my major itch to do it myself!

CASE STUDY: David C. Novak, Executive Chairman and Ex-CEO of Yum!

David Novak saw himself more as the chief teaching officer rather than CEO of Yum! (housing famous global brands such as KFC and Pizza Hut) and believes that *recognition* is the foundation for motivation – which is the only way to make big things happen and be sustainable. David was awarded the prestigious CEO of the Year award in 2012, joining a list of luminaries that includes legends such as Bill Gates and Jack Welch. I was fortunate enough to talk to David about his philosophies concerning great leadership, and how he has brought these to life in his career.

David has a very clear and challenging mantra, which is that all leaders need to see the position of leadership as a *privilege*, and not an entitlement. Furthermore, giving out regular recognition is one of the privileges (and requirements) of good leadership. David explains:

'As a leader you can make or break someone's day depending on how you treat them, and you should never underestimate the impact, both good and bad, you can have on others as a leader. People usually leave places because they don't get along with their boss (that's why we develop leadership coaches, not bosses, at Yum!). In fact, viewing yourself as a "boss" is old school management and a thing of the past (makes you a relic).'

He continues: 'Recognition is not just around pointing out people doing the right things, it's also about being clear if they are doing the wrong things – so it's recognition of both the *right* behaviours and the *wrong* behaviours that drives the desired culture. By being clear what the high standards look like, you can coach people for better behaviours and set the standards for people to aspire to. The mindset of leadership should be that you value the opportunity, treasure it and are grateful for it, rather than a mindset of feeling entitled to something if you are a leader.'

David has a philosophy of taking the business very seriously, but not taking yourselves too seriously. He has had his best successes from creating an environment of appreciation and fun, and finds that this leads to people making the best decisions because they're in a state of happiness and high gratitude. On the flip side, David observes that you make your worst decisions when you are angry and not having fun – very true!

Yum! Is now in 120 countries and prides itself on creating an inspiring and replicable environment of fun, a powerful culture, high standards, strong appreciation and continuous growth, all of which help keep the very best people and attract the very best people to join.

David subscribes to the view that people leave companies for two main reasons: 1) their boss, and 2) they don't get appreciated. Therefore the whole culture at Yum! revolves around investing in the quality of management behaviours and an environment of appreciation and value.

One of the best instances of this was when Yum! built up the KFC franchise base in Russia from scratch in one of the toughest environments possible – one in which their direct competitors, including McDonalds, had struggled. Yum! managed to create an incredible team, and sustained it all through focus on great management and lots of recognition. This model continues to be replicated worldwide, a recent example being the enormous growth of KFC and Pizza Hut in Africa, where the recognition model continues to work regardless of any cultural and diversity differences.

The recruitment process at Yum! is absolutely vital to the company's future success and everyone they hire has to share the same values. When David stepped up to Executive Chairman, the CEO role was taken up by Greg Creed, who had been developed internally and demonstrated he could not only live the culture, but drive it as a leader. Greg continues to lead and embody the legacy that David created when he was CEO.

As David says, 'It's important that you let people know that you're watching them and showing them that they matter, because if people don't think what they do matters, then you won't get the effort or commitment that you need to drive great companies. You cannot sustain a great business without a great leader, and recognition is the key lever of building an A-Team.'

David reflected on a time from his early career when he was running PepsiCo's operations and would conduct roundtables with people when he visited the warehouses and the bottling plants. One morning, he was with a group of salesmen and asked them about merchandising. They all started talking (raving even) about an employee named Bob, who was sitting at the end of the table. Bob had apparently taught them more about merchandising than anybody else. He was the best they'd ever worked with. David remembers looking down to the end of the table to see that Bob was crying.

'Why are you crying?' he asked, to which Bob answered, 'Well, I'm crying because I've been in this company for 47 years and I never knew people felt this way about me.'

Here was a person who was obviously the best at what he did – people looked up to him. David thought, What a waste! Bob hadn't known that people appreciated him so much. Imagine what he could have done for the company if he had been properly recognised, but for 47 years he had never had the opportunity to shine. David promised himself that if he ever had a chance to run a company, he was going to make recognition the number one value.

As David moved up the ranks, he developed his own recognition awards which he would give to his teams, and he made the time to celebrate when they really achieved great things together. Every time he did so, whether by saying thank you to an individual or recognising people in a group, it was always appreciated and it motivated people.

When he became President of KFC at PepsiCo, he famously started awarding floppy (rubber) chickens along with a small cheque as a token of recognition. As he explains, 'People started crying when I gave it [the award] to them and were incredibly motivated by it. It ignited performance because people respond to recognition. When you recognise people, it says that you're watching. It says that what they do matters.' Intuitively David always knew this. He formalised it with a more structured awards scheme across the business, and it took off like wildfire!

These actions and experiences have shaped David's approach to leadership, which he carried on at Yum! Today, every leader in Yum! has their own individual approach to recognition awards, so it's not just David who gives out the recognition now. It's all of the leadership, all with their own personality.

EXPERT VIEW: Graeme Codrington, CEO of TomorrowTodayGlobal

Dr Graeme Codrington, expert on the future of work and author of the best-selling book on understanding different generations *Mind the Gap*, agrees that the act of shining a light on people around you is one of the most important ways a leader can motivate everyone, and particularly younger generations. As Graeme explains:

'Today's young people want to feel empowered and want their work to make a real difference, more so than previous generations. An easy way to do this is to provide a sense of autonomy for talented young people, allowing them to lead projects and assignments they have been given. The less experience they have, the smaller the task should be, but nevertheless stepping back and letting them lead can be hugely motivational for younger people especially.'

Graeme remembers an instance of this at a legal firm in London, 'Professional service firms are going through significant changes in their leadership styles. Senior partners can no longer ignore talent development issues, nor treat their junior staff not much better than slaves. Especially in legal firms, senior partners now need to generate business for the firm and build teams of junior staff to deliver results to clients. These are often not skills that have been valued before.'

This particular legal firm was losing a lot of talented young lawyers, who either left to move into other industries or were poached by other legal firms. Through a series of developmental workshops Graeme ran, he discovered that, of the reasons they chose to go to other firms, the top issue was that their manager (typically a senior partner) did not give them a chance to grow and develop. It required both a changed mindset and a new set of skills for senior partners to begin to adjust their behaviours and, in particular, let go of the more hierarchical diet that they had historically been brought up on. Another positive feature that came from the workshop findings was the deployment of a new measurement system of what good management involved, which carried both rewards and consequences.

Graeme and his team at TomorrowTodayGlobal have seen this theme over and over again in the companies they work with: today's young people are not just younger versions of their older managers.

'They have different expectations of what the world of work should be like. They respond best to leaders who have higher EQ (Emotional Quotient), who are less commanding and more participative and democratic, who help to develop them in their careers and lives, and who are strong in the *Loving Leadership* techniques that Richard has covered in his book.'

Shine a Light Summary Checklist: 10 Big Things

1. There is a difference between recognising someone and embarrassing them – take care!

2. Creating a habit of observing and rewarding great work creates deep trust and motivation.

3. The more timely you can be with praise, the best chance of repeatability by the recipient.

4. Always prepare in detail for more formal recognition events – it's powerful if it's personal.

5. Be on the look-out for future talent. You can find it anywhere if you look hard enough.

6. Build winning teams with a mixture of talents and experiences and allow all to shine.

7. Let go of as many things as you can if you have team members capable of stepping up.

8. Never, ever, assume people know how much they are valued – tell them, regularly.

9. It's equally important to address the wrong behaviours and request improvements.

10. Remove road blocks to give people the best chance of succeeding and building confidence.

CHAPTER 5:

CREATE MAGIC
MOMENTS

'I have learned that people will forget what you said, people will forget what you did, but people will never forget how you made them feel.'

Maya Angelou

Surprise people

Everybody likes a surprise. Even people who say they don't like surprises actually do. It's just that they worry it might not be exactly what they want, so it's easier to default to saying 'I don't like surprises'. If you make sure it's a nice surprise, something they were not expecting but couldn't fail to be happy with, then the concept of a nice surprise becomes something meaningful to the individual, and can create a memory that will last forever.

The surprise doesn't have to be big. Or expensive. A few years ago, when Jersey was experiencing one of its hottest summers ever, the air conditioning in Head Office there failed. Potentially this was a source of unrest, and indeed started to become so. The office became far warmer than usual, people were complaining, accusations of blame were rife, and the atmosphere was generally deteriorating.

Then one of the executives suppressed the near-mutiny with a simple action (an inspired phone call, actually) that had nothing to do with fixing the air conditioning. Following a familiar happy ringing tune outside the building, an ice cream van arrived. At the same time, a light-hearted internal note went out saying that every member of staff was welcome to go outside and get a free ice cream, and that the van would stay until everyone had chosen. With around 150 people in the office, the cost was no more than £300, but the element of surprise created a disproportionately positive reaction that actually gelled the workforce. Conversations included:

- Hey, what flavour did you go for?

- What, you got two, you pig!

- What a great thing to do. The Directors wouldn't have done this at my last company

- I could get used to this. Let's hope they don't fix the air con for a few days

- Maybe it isn't so bad inside after all. I'll just take a few layers off

- Aren't we lucky with this beautiful weather? Can't wait to get to the beach later

And, several years on, this small gesture is still remembered. It's used to support the fact that the leaders really do care about staff and are human.

However, a note of caution: the point of this real story is that it was not about the ice cream. It was the thought, the timing, and the element of a nice surprise. It's all about reacting as a leader and doing the best thing in the circumstances, and that doesn't mean that you always have to fix the immediate problem. Every situation lends itself to different appropriate actions, which needs proactivity, thoughtfulness, and creativity to result in a positive reaction, so please don't go and hire an ice cream van and expect the same results!

Remember little details

In any relationship, it's the little touches here and there that show you care. One of the most impactful things you can do for anyone is to remember (and recognise) things relating to them as a person, showing that they are more than just a worker. They exist as a human, have a purpose, are valued, special, and part of a team.

If this doesn't come naturally to you, try turning it into a task and keep small memory joggers where you note down key information about people. For example:

- **Their family:** This is a really big one – massive bonus points to any leader who can remember the names and ages of people's children; double points if you know what school they go to and the sort of stuff they are into; and triple points if you also know what someone's wife/husband/partner's name is, and what they do.

- **What people like and don't like:** How do people take their tea/coffee? Do they like a Sauvignon or a Merlot? Chocolate cake or lemon sponge? Creme Eggs or Toblerone? Are they allergic to wheat? If you ask, observe, engage in conversations with people, and do a bit of socialising, these things come up, and if you ever remember them spontaneously, it can make people feel very special. Imagine how you would feel if you were having a bad morning and someone spontaneously put a double shot latte and a pain au chocolate by your side, knowing it was your favourite combination.

The list could go on and on, but here are some more hints of things to help get you started:

- Birthdays of anyone you regularly work with. Most people love a 'Happy birthday!'

- Baby due dates for any mums and dads-to-be

- Pets (what type, how many, and names). People love their pets, and 48% of UK households have at least one pet

- Special events people are planning, e.g. running a marathon, playing at a concert, etc.

- Holidays: when they go, where they're going and with whom, when they return

- Exam dates, professional qualifications, training courses

- Any health issues, e.g. doctor's appointments, forthcoming operations, etc.

- Sick relatives, and any demanding responsibilities relating to them

- Where they live (now) and where they originate from (childhood)

- What school, university, college they went to, and what courses they studied

- What other jobs they have done in the past, and for what companies

- Long service with the company

Even if you have forgotten that they were on the horizon, marking these events as private appointments in your calendar will ensure they pop up on the day as prompts.

Wayne Mullen, Executive Leadership Director at King, brings this technique to life in a memorable example:

'I worked with a Global Head of Audit who used to remember little details about people. When talking with you he would refer to your outside interests or perhaps ask about your partner or children by name. It was part of how he connected and created rapport with people – it made people feel significant in his presence. As a result he had a team that would go to the ends of the earth for him.'

Be spontaneous

The spirit of spontaneity has been ebbing away from workplaces all over the world over the last 20 years. It seems that everywhere we look, there are reasons not to make a decision and notes of caution about doing anything without due consideration. A few companies have managed to buck the trend and drive cultures of spontaneity and fun, but far more have become boring.

We find ourselves in a world of policies-gone-mad, where managers and leaders are always being conditioned to check before they act. We are surrounded by extensive corporate policies and procedures, discrimination laws, handbooks, red tape, anti-bribery and other new legislations, internal governance, approval committees, authorisation matrices, and the possible consequences of falling foul of these. This has prevented many people from retaining a basic level of confidence to act spontaneously if an opportunity to do something special or say something nice arises, and unfortunately that means that these unique moments pass by.

Here is my advice: if the inspiration takes you to do something, say thank you to someone, or celebrate something good, then *do it*. Trust yourself and your instincts, because you are a uniquely designed machine which is a natural blend of genetics, knowledge, skills and experience, and you do know the right thing to do. Don't worry if it's 'not very 'corporate' – everyone wants a bit of fun in their life. Any decent company will back you to the hilt as a leader if you make a decision that creates a magic moment based on spontaneity – as long as the reward is within reason, of course.

For that split second when the time is right, don't worry about the things mentioned in the mesh of corporate red tape: expenses policies, travel policies, entertainment policies, gift registers, etc. Just do it. And if the mood-hoovers and the corporate risk brigade berate you for it, and your manager frowns and expresses his/her disappointment, get out of the organisation – it will fail in the long run with this attitude. Ask yourself, 'Did it do any harm?'

In essence, spontaneity is simply your instinct. Your gut feeling. A chemical surge to action without time for logical or rational analysis. In the vast majority of cases your instinct will prove to be true. Never fear acting on it – you will be placing yourself and your reputation at far more risk by not listening to your instinct. And this has evolved through thousands of years of the human race to ensure that we survive and thrive through loving, providing, giving and achieving.

I recently witnessed first-hand a leader spontaneously create a truly memorable moment. The scenario was this: a sales manager had just won the biggest contract in a company's history after a painstaking three-year tendering process and was in a taxi heading back to the airport to fly home. I was with the Managing Director of the company when he took the call from the sales manager. Without pausing for breath, the MD said:

'Fantastic, I am so pleased. Upgrade yourself to business class and get a bottle of champagne on the company for the journey home. Well done!'

Yes, this broke a number of policies, not least travel and expenses (business class was excluded across the whole company at the time). Technically speaking the MD shouldn't have promoted the consumption of alcohol for a team member during work time either, but ask yourself – was this a good leadership decision? Too right it was. Bravo to the MD, and the sales manager will never forget the spontaneity and the timely reward. Can you imagine how special they felt on the way home knowing that their reward was something exceptional?

Trust your instincts and be spontaneous!

CASE STUDY: Beatrice Tollman, Founder and President of Red Carnation Hotels

Red Carnation Hotels was voted the #2 Best Midsize Company to work for in 2014, an incredible accolade achieved through the foundations of making employees feel individually special.

'Red Carnation Hotels is my passion and I live it 24 hours a day, 365 days a year, no matter where I am in the world,' says Beatrice Tollman, who has been running the company for over 60 years. 'In the hotel industry no day is ever the same, and I still get the same enjoyment from giving our guests value, comfort, beautiful rooms, delicious food and – above all – the best service.'

Beatrice's staff give her an 87% positive score for being an inspiring leader (just one other boss ranked higher in the UK Best Companies survey). They feel she runs the organisation based on sound moral principles. (90%, first place on the midsize list).

Beatrice's philosophy is that great service brings guests back to stay, and to give brilliant service you need employees who really care. This can only be achieved, in her opinion, if you treat your employees well – both in and out of work. She strives hard to ensure that people are looked after, cared about, treated as individuals, feel supported and valued, have their welfare considered and are thanked. These are very much the same principles which are enjoyed by the guests staying in the hotels.

What makes her unique is that as Red Carnation Hotels' founder and president, she visits all the hotels regularly, creating endless magic moments for employees by:

- Knowing many staff by name, remembering personal things about them, and greeting them warmly when doing hotel visits

- Finding a way to keep in touch with every member of staff on a daily basis through some form of communication that shows that she is there, she cares, and is available for them

- Sending everyone in the company an individually tailored Christmas present

- Offering bespoke training, development, qualifications and experiences that help staff achieve as much as they can from their careers and their lives

- Anyone mentioned on TripAdvisor, or in a written guest comment, receives a personalised thank you from her (she reads every comment every day from every global location without fail)

- Taking an active interest in everyone she meets, and they know and feel this to be the case

- Throwing a memorable annual staff party to celebrate achievement and reward numerous employees, with Beatrice thanking everyone

In my interview with Beatrice (which was over the phone as she was spending time with staff at the Hôtel D'Angleterre in Geneva), I asked her to expand on a couple of these magic moments, and was amazed at the detail that the process entailed. What was clear is that she cuts no corners, takes no short cuts, and runs one of the most empowering organisations I have come across by setting the example of genuine care for others through her own actions.

She started by talking me through the annual party, which is actually called the 'Staff Appreciation Party' and is the highlight of the year both for her and the staff. There are over 2,000 staff across 17 hotels in the RCH Group worldwide, and well over 1,000 of these make the annual party. Such is its success and reputation that Beatrice explained how they have outgrown the Savoy and London Hilton, moving to Grosvenor House as a larger venue to accommodate everyone.

Red Carnation employees come from all over the world to attend what is clearly a memorable and prestigious event – and it's an even bigger magic moment for the majority of the employees because they are in low-paid blue-collar roles, so to attend a ball and be wined and dined and recognised is an incredible experience. It is also an opportunity for staff from all 17 hotel locations to meet and mix, so chefs from different countries talk to each other, as do receptionists, housekeepers and gardeners, and they compare what it's like to work in different environments.

The evening is also awash with recognition awards, from 'best general manager' to 'best chef', and even 'most helpful person' – there are categories for all, anyone can win a prize, there is no hierarchy, everyone is equally important and valued. Many of the nominations come via monthly tea parties which are run in every hotel – magic moments in themselves. At the Staff Appreciation Party, Beatrice always books a fantastic band with dancing girls and memorable catering, and puts on an amazing theme, making it a spectacular occasion. The prize winners even get to dance with the band, holding their awards and being sung to, feeling really special.

I asked Beatrice about her famous 'individual Christmas presents'. Surely it would not be possible for some 2,000 people to get something genuinely individual that she had personally planned and organised. Well, I was wrong with my assumption! Beatrice actively updates personal information on all 2,000 Red Carnation employees, including what they do, what they like, and what they have received in previous years. She then gives every member of staff a signed Christmas card along with a present that is unique to them – such is the level of care and attention to detail.

So this is in no way a corporate exercise that is delegated behind the scenes; it's a very real gesture from the heart. Amazing. But then again, it starts to explain why her workforce feel the way they do –they know it is absolutely genuine. I asked Beatrice how she could possibly achieve this task on top of everything else, and the answer was that she simply doesn't stop working pretty much every waking minute, seven days a week. Because she cares, she starts early enough with the process to make sure it's finished in time for Christmas.

She explained how it is all worth it. The staff are so grateful, and in return they give Red Carnation Hotels wonderful service. From all the guest feedback, the biggest standout area is the people, and to quote a recent report that Beatrice received from a satisfied customer:

'My husband and I are lucky to be global travellers who have stayed in the best hotels from Rome to Paris to New York, and I can honestly say that your staff are the best in the world.'

Beatrice shared that it was not easy staying on top of all the emails and letters of thanks she gets from her staff in response to the things she does. She had just received one from a pastry chef in Cape Town, SA, who had taken Beatrice up on her personal offer for him to have a meal with his partner at the Taste Kitchen, an establishment famous for its pastries. Not a cheap night out! This had clearly been a really magic moment for the chef, who was so thankful.

Beatrice is living proof that genuinely caring for your staff, and making them feel special, pays.

EXPERT VIEW: Shaun Smith, Founder of Smith & Co, Author of *Bold*

Shaun Smith is a renowned global leader in creating compelling customer experiences that achieve brand differentiation and loyalty, his biggest recent success being the amazing turnaround of Premier Inn's brand. He is co-author of five acclaimed business books, of which *Bold – How to be Brave in Business and Win* was awarded CMI's 2012 Management e-book of the Year. His current focus is on how consumers are increasingly favouring brands that have a purpose beyond profit, and it is only possible to create these brands from the inside out by first creating a purpose that is powerfully embodied by the workforce.

As Shaun explains, 'Nowhere is the notion of creating "Magic Moments" and surprising people more powerful than in the realm of customer and employee experience. In this world of CRM, processes and Health and Safety, we have become conditioned to expect most experiences as a customer to be efficient and effective, but not very memorable. The good thing is that most brands now provide service experiences that are reasonably consistent and certainly of a higher quality than was the norm ten years ago. But somehow they lack a little bit of spontaneity: that human touch that makes them memorable. The best brands realise this and design experiences that allow their people to improvise within brand guidelines to create a distinctive customer experience.

'In order to surprise customers – in a positive way – with unexpected magic moments, you need to create a different kind of leadership style in your organisation. Most organisations in our experience operate on 'Loose/Tight' principles. They are loose when it comes to telling their people what their brand purpose is, the brand values and the kind of emotional experience they wish to have. But they are tight when it comes to standard operating procedures and processes. So a call centre agent will typically know that the Average Call Handling Time target is 45 seconds but not how the customer should feel about the brand as a result of it.

'We advocate switching these around so that leaders communicate the brand purpose, values and desired customer experience to employees and give them a bit more freedom to decide how to innovate and create those unexpected magic moments that can turn a routine transaction into a memorable experience. By reinforcing the purpose and values through creating some magic moments for your own staff, you empower and motivate them to pass the feeling on by having the same attitude with the customers – you will be surprised at how innovative your people can be.

'For example, there is a story we tell in our new book about Virgin Atlantic – *On Purpose – Delivering a Branded Customer Experience People Love*. In the days before high-tech seat-back entertainment, airlines would have a drop down screen in the main cabin and schedule movies to follow the meal service. Virgin Atlantic decided to make this a proper movie experience and serve ice creams just like at the cinema. That was a magic moment at that time because no other airline served ice cream on their aircraft due to the lack of freezers on board. Virgin solved the problem by packing the ice cream in dry ice.

'One of the Virgin flight attendants took the creation of this unique, memorable customer experience one stage further. In the galley, before serving the ice creams she would smear some ice cream around her mouth. As she walked down the cabin with the ice cream tray, she would say loudly, "People tell me these ice creams are delicious, but I'm on a diet and never touch them. Enjoy!"

'As passengers looked up, they saw the ice cream around her mouth and the smile on her face and a ripple of laughter would follow her down the aisle. Other passengers looked up to see what people were laughing at and joined in.

'The story rippled around the world, becoming viral. People who had never flown Virgin heard about it, and perhaps, when they had to book a trans-Atlantic flight and choose between Virgin and their competitors, they were influenced to book Virgin because they wanted that human touch. So much of airline travel today is heavily regulated.

'How much does an ice cream cost compared with a new aircraft? How could any training programme or service standards manual have prescribed that behaviour to the company's employees? How much interest did that viral story generate compared with an expensive advertising campaign? Consumers (and employees) remember an emotional experience more than a functional one. It was a great manifestation of the Virgin Atlantic's brand values of fun, entertainment, irreverence and innovation, and serves to reinforce the brand positioning.

Create Magic Moments Summary Checklist: 10 Big Things

1. Everybody likes a nice surprise, even those who say they don't.

2. The best surprises are often down to thought and timing, not money.

3. Remember little details that are unique to someone, and tailor the surprise to match.

4. Keep lists of things that you know are important to people, and check from time to time.

5. Trust your instincts and be spontaneous – break rules and policies if you need to!

6. Build time into your day to think proactively of ways to delight and surprise others.

7. The more personal you can make recognition and thanks, the deeper the connection.

8. Think about events and experiences rather than gifts – memories last forever.

9. Create moments of personal recognition that thank people for particular efforts.

10. Make a big effort to get to know people, socialise, ask questions and show interest.

CHAPTER 6:

REALLY LISTEN

'You cannot truly listen to anyone and do anything else at the same time.'

M. Scott Peck

Get to know the whole person

Listening is an example of a fundamental life skill that is simple to describe, but for some people it is hugely difficult (if not nigh on impossible) ever to do properly. In the last chapter we looked at the importance of remembering little details, which subsequently allow you to create magic moments for others, be it staff or colleagues. As much as this can be done with a bit of focus and task management (i.e. keeping a note of such things), it requires the skill of really *listening* in the first place to hear and understand what people are saying.

One of the biggest shortcomings not just of leaders, but of the human race, is that we are pre-programmed to hear what we want to hear, and are often mentally preparing what we are going to say next. In the life of a leader, faced with a data-heavy, time-poor environment, it actually takes a lot of skill, effort and self-control to devote time to listening. However, don't despair – exceptional listening skills are rare (so don't beat yourself up too much) and are developed through a combination of mind control and practice. Everyone can get better with effort.

The Oxford English Dictionary defines the act of listening as '*to make an effort to hear something. To pay attention*'. Therefore to be listening completely, it is actually not possible to be doing anything else. In the world of multitasking, listening breaks the rule. Imagine yourself driving and listening to your passenger talking about something important. You may achieve 50% focus on them, but it is impossible to listen and focus 100% without crashing the car (please don't try and prove me wrong!).

So herein lies a challenge for leaders – how to create an appropriate environment conducive not just to hearing what is the 'low hanging fruit' (i.e. easy to remember and fits your agenda), but also to appreciate and understand the whole person talking to you. By listening to the whole person, you are picking up not just what they say, but how they say it (i.e. the intent and meaning and truth in the statements).

Elizabeth Kuhnke, executive coach and author of *Persuasion and Influence For Dummies*, agrees with the importance of this technique. She says:

'When you listen with empathy, engaging your ears, eyes, and heart in a desire to capture the full meaning of the speaker's message, you're indicating that you value that person. When people feel valued their motivation and morale sky rockets, resulting in positive relationships and enhanced performance.

'Take Liz, for example, who works for a financial services organisation and is held in high regard by her boss, clients and colleagues. Although she likes her job and the people she works with, Liz was feeling disgruntled and undervalued, having discovered that the men in the company who were doing the same job as she did were being paid more.

'During their quarterly review, Liz's boss, Karyn, noticed that Liz spoke less than usual. She also observed that Liz's face was flushed and that she struggled to maintain eye contact. By gently asking probing questions, acknowledging what she was observing, and letting Liz speak without judging or interrupting, Karyn opened the door for Liz to express her feelings.

'Having been unaware of the pay discrepancy, Karyn promised that she would look into it, which she did. As a result of Karyn's active listening skills, she was able to identify and act upon the source of Liz's grievance, averting a potential problem for the firm. In addition, because Liz felt listened to and heard, she renewed her efforts and continues to produce outstanding results. And, she got the financial package she wanted.'

Try this easy test to see how well you actually know the whole person based on people who work with you. Pick a couple of people in your team, maybe a peer in another department, or even your boss or direct reports, then answer the following four questions in as much detail as you can:

- Why do they come to work and do the job they do?

- What do they love doing outside of work?

- What are their aspirations and plans for the future?

- What are the names and occupations/schools of their closest family members?

How did you do? If you breezed through with flying colours then you are in the upper quartile of listeners, so well done. If you didn't do so well, ask yourself why. It might be one or more of the following three reasons:

- Did you ask the questions to find out in the first place (maybe you lacked curiosity)?

- Did you really listen to the answers when you were talking to them? Were you possibly distracted?

- Did you concentrate on relevant information flying around every day, or were you 'not in the moment'?

I tested this out at the time of writing with several people in my team and around the business, and they were amazed and slightly embarrassed at what they didn't know. Many admitted that they didn't know the name of their colleagues' wives/husbands or children. Many had no idea what close colleagues enjoyed outside work. Several didn't know anything about others' backgrounds: where they live, where they come from. Some had forgotten people's surnames, and one person didn't even know that the person they described had actually left the company almost a year earlier!

However, when asked at the start of this small experiment, 'Would you consider that you know this person fairly well?', they had all answered yes. When I asked the questions, they soon realised that knowing who someone is, in terms of what they look like and sound like, what they do in work, what office banter you might have at a veneer level, and what things they are working on, often bears little significance to *who they really are* (i.e. the 'whole person').

You can begin changing this from today. By simply listening with greater focus, intensity and concentration, you can start to understand the whole person at a deeper level, namely:

- What are they motivated and driven by?

- What are their values and ethics?

- How does their job fit into their wider life goals and ambitions?

- Who and what is most important to them – their personal priorities?

- What makes them happy and what makes them sad?

- What do they need from you as a leader (and what don't they need from you)?

- What type of work do and don't they enjoy?

- What are their broader skills and abilities?

- What are their career ambitions and personal potential?

Next time you are in a dialogue with someone whom you are building a relationship with, ask yourself, 'Am I really listening to hear and understand?' If you can make this shift, and start exploring and remembering these things, you can be an incredibly powerful leader to them.

Show that you have heard them

Ask yourself the following question, and give it some hard thought:

'How do *you know* when someone has listened to you and heard you?'

You probably came up with things that described what it would look and feel like. Perhaps the recipient of your message is nodding, maintaining good eye contact, focussing only on you and not being distracted by other tasks. Giving you positive affirmations through their body language and gestures. Clarifying your answers, asking further questions directly relevant to your responses, maybe taking notes, building on what you are saying, summarising the key points. Showing an emotional response at an appropriate time, be it smiling, frowning, laughing. Not rushing you. Not butting in. Making commitments to take action, etc.

OK, that's good. Feels good. So now ask yourself the following, again with some hard thought:

'What do *you do* when someone is talking to you?'

Let's be truthful. In a typical interaction, be it one-to-one or in a group, are you sometimes:

- Distracted by your phone or other device vibrating?

- Not always looking at the person speaking?

- Caught out when you are asked a question on the content of the conversation?

- Trying to multitask, e.g. getting some data ready for the next meeting?

- Focussing on what *you* are going to say next?

- Worrying about other things that are on today's horizon?

- Losing your concentration at times, maybe daydreaming?

- Forgetful of some elements of what was said?

- Finishing people's sentences for them (so annoying for the recipient)?

- Interrupting and cutting over people when they are talking?

- Thinking I really haven't got time for this?

- Secretly annoyed and frustrated by the interruption?

Unless you are in the top tier of listeners, I can guess your answers, and they will certainly not be perfect. I can honestly tell you that neither are mine! The problem with not completely listening (either one or both parties) is that the *quality* of the conversation really suffers. As a result, any outcome from the interaction will be limited. Conversely, high-quality conversations (great listening) will drive deeper relationships and better results. This very tangible benefit is covered in more detail by Wayne Clarke at the end of this chapter with an amazing example.

If you show one or more signs to someone that you are not really listening, then turn that round for a minute and step into their shoes – how do you think the person speaking feels? Do they feel listened to, valued and important? And because you are their leader, what impact do you think this might have? How might that affect their engagement, behaviour and motivation? Is this how you want them to feel?

Of course not!

Jon Lavelle, international leadership and negotiation skills trainer, agrees that listening, and in particular showing people that you are *genuinely* hearing what they are saying, is one of the most powerful leadership techniques and life skills that any person can develop. He suggests six tips, gleaned during his career, to becoming a real 'power listener':

1. Listen for understanding rather than simply to respond. You can tell when someone has stopped listening and is thinking of what they want to say next. They appear preoccupied, pounce on any pause or talk over you. By listening for understanding, you'll keep an open demeanour and posture, and avoid giving any signals that may indicate you're closed to the information/message.

2. When feeding back what you've heard, pause, question for clarification as you go, and finish by asking if you've understood correctly.

3. Reflect back feelings as well as facts; people are human, they want to know you are too.

4. Indicate a willingness to re-listen if your interpretation proves incorrect.

5. If you've listened and decide to hold your ground, or take another course of action, at least explain your reasons. Listening is not about acquiescing; it's about genuinely showing that you've taken others' perspectives into account before coming to conclusions and making a decision.

6. Remember, the last word in listen is 'ten'. Listening is 10 times more powerful, in the long run, than talking. Sometimes less is more, and if you rearrange the letters in the word 'listen' it spells 'silent'!

As with so many of the high impact leadership techniques covered in this book, listening is very simple to grasp but hard to execute. This is particularly the case with deep listening because it's much more mentally demanding to listen than to speak, so it's something that you must actively work on to keep the skill well honed. The rewards will be great, so give it a go.

Oh, and you can also try it with relationships at home, with surprisingly beneficial results!

Take action on what people say

One of the biggest influences on levels of staff engagement is related not just to people feeling listened to by leaders, but by the *leaders taking action* as a result.

Although accepting and embracing that listening (as opposed to talking) is a major step forward on building relationships, as is validating/reflecting back, the circle of communication is not yet complete. In a lot of cases, leaders will ultimately be judged on the quality of the subsequent *actions* taken showing that they not only listen, but are committed to helping improve things in some shape or form.

Action does not have to be something major and grandiosely visible to everyone, such as a big change programme or creating a new framework for a particular theme. In many cases, it can be just a small thing that completes the loop of 'ask-listen-action' feedback.

In fact, sometimes the leader might take action that the employee doesn't even know about but which makes their life that little bit easier and more enjoyable. Maybe one day the employee will conclude that there must have been an intervention that helped smooth the path.

A major failing I have observed in leadership across many organisations is that leaders ask, perhaps listen, but don't act. Examples include saying that you don't have budget to make improvements (well, why ask people what improvements could be made then?), or doing something completely different even if the mood of the frontline workforce is telling you otherwise (again, why ask them if you won't listen?). This is professional suicide. Great leaders have faith in their workers to know the best answers and solutions, and also the backbone to deliver improvements. Hiding behind politics and lack of budget is simply not acceptable. There is always a way. No excuses.

The very successful series *Undercover Boss* has many examples of leaders taking action on what people say. It's a great concept, where the CEO of the organisation goes undercover into one or more of the customer facing roles of the company. They typically spend a week experiencing the life of someone who is required to be the visible demonstration of everything the company is trying to achieve and the brand experience it is aiming to deliver and reinforce.

In one episode, the CEO of a famous car manufacturer spent time in one of their dealerships, working in the garage and on the service desk. As part of his training, he was required to learn how to carry out a 30 point service check within 15 minutes, as the branch was measured against a baseline of four service checks per person per hour. It soon became clear that what was being asked of the staff was impossible, no matter how competent the individual. In fact, the company's best mechanic could not achieve the full check in the allotted time. This was putting enormous strain on the staff, who were required either to work a lot of overtime (without pay) or put the brand promise at risk by missing out some of the service checks.

The CEO listened, observed, and took action – when he revealed his true identify later in the TV programme, he doubled the amount of time allowed for service checks across all dealerships, making no compromise on service quality. The workforce felt truly listened to, and it has had a major impact on their motivation, customer service and stress-reduction.

The concept of demonstrating listening through appropriate action is not a recent discovery – in fact, far from it. Listening and delivering has defined great leaders throughout history, separating them from the pack. One of Benjamin Franklin's most cited quotes from the late 1700s is '*Speak little, and do much*'. He certainly had the right idea.

CASE STUDY: Allan Leighton, Ex-CEO of Asda, and Chairman of Royal Mail

I had the pleasure of engaging with Allan for a piece of leadership consultancy a few years ago, and witnessed first-hand the motivational power that he can impart to others. We were approaching our major customer event of the year – the iconic Jersey Live music festival (which JT sponsors every year) where our company leaders were going to be hosting over 200 local dignitaries, politicians, executives and key strategic global partners and gold customers.

This was an event that had previously been marketing-led with just the CEO and Sales Directors doing the hosting. We had taken the decision to get our top 30 leaders below the executive team to step up in terms of their profile, client visibility and supporting relationships and service, regardless of their role and function, and everyone was asked to attend and host this high profile event as a representative of JT.

Allan got the leadership group really fired up and confident for the day ahead, and played hard on the theme of 'brand ambassadors': the part every leader can play in the embodiment of a brand and what it means. However, there was a twist. We were expecting to glean a heap of material about all the impressive things we could say at these events to impress our VIPs, but this was not forthcoming. Allan focused on something far more powerful – the art of listening. He facilitated a number of scenarios that were all about getting the guests to feel comfortable and relaxed, which was all about getting *them* to talk.

We soon realised that the barometer of success was not what we managed to say to the guests, but the quality of questions and active listening that led to what they said to us. On a ratio, we were encouraged to aim for 80:20 in the guests' favour. This was a very valuable lesson. We spent the evening researching the guests' backgrounds and thinking of great questions to ask them rather than working on what we would say to the guests. The event was a huge success, not just for the happy guests, but also for Allan, whose greatly talented son played at the festival. A proud moment for him.

In his book *On Leadership*, Allan describes the 'Art of Communication' of a great leader as being far more about listening and taking actions rather than talking and giving actions. Many of Allan's experiences reinforce the observations made in this 'Really Listen' chapter. As a case in point, one of the largest chunks of Allan's time is currently spent dealing with his 'Ask Allan' scheme as Chairman of the Royal Mail.

This two-way direct feedback line generates over 400 emails a day, and Allan commits to responding to all of them within 24 hours whenever this is practicable. It's an enormous undertaking, but the result is that the workforce really feel heard as Allan prioritises his time to put their needs first.

Allan is also well-known for casually plotting his way round the guts of the organisations he has worked for – the shop floors, depots, call centres, processing plants and factories. One of the most used and successful questions he asks many people he meets on these travels is:

'If there are a couple of things I could "magic" for you, what would they be?'

Allan explains that this is when he finds out what the real issues are. 'The subjects that concern people are always at the top of their minds; they carry them around with them. If I ask anyone what are the two things that bug them most about their company or their home life, they'll rattle them off straight away.'

When asked about the requirement for greater listening skills in the wider world of communications, Allan points to a particular bugbear of his, namely presentations delivered 'at' audiences with slide projectors and no interaction or participation, even worse when each bullet point 'swoops' in.

Allan explains, 'Some great communication skills trainers teach people the minutiae of presentations, but often miss the most vital point. It is far more important to have an actual conversation with your audience, engage with them and understand what they want to get out of the exercise than to attempt to knock them out with well-prepared purple prose.'

In summary, communication has to be a two-way street or else it either hasn't actually taken place or you have no idea if it has or not. The constant flow of ideas back and forth in an organisation is its life blood, and should be stimulated by leaders at every opportunity.

EXPERT VIEW: Wayne Clarke, Founding Partner at The Global Growth Institute

I started working with Wayne Clarke seven years ago when I first experienced the Best Companies Times Top 100 Methodology for Staff Engagement, something that is fully embedded within JT as a stretching benchmark when aspiring to be a truly great place to work. What immediately struck me was Wayne's absolute passion for personal, team and organisational improvement through leadership and relationships. He has worked at the very highest global levels with corporate, government and not-for-profit boards, and boils down the ultimate driver of success, mediocrity or failure to the quality of conversations that occur between people that lead to key decisions being made. Wayne brings, as he puts it, the 'power of great dialogue' to life as follows:

'Great relationships, unless you use telepathy (and there aren't many people who are very skilled at this), are usually the outcome of great interactions, mostly conversations. Sounds simple. What we talk about, and how we talk about it, has the power to create deep, enduring relationships, as does our ability to be self-aware about the impact we're having on others.

'Through the quality of their conversations and interactions, individuals in an organisation have a strong effect on their colleagues', customers' and the general public's perception of the organisation and what it stands for, and its performance. Each interaction and each conversation may seem irrelevant at the time, but in the grand scheme of things we know it's the small, quick interactions that can often have the biggest effect on organisations. Why? Because they make people "feel" something.

'The thing is, some people are really self-aware about how they make others feel; some haven't a clue about how they come across; and some (luckily a minority) don't care at all! Quality conversation isn't about a deep transcendental exchange on the nature of our existence. It could be if you're that way inclined, but it's more about the regular, quick interactions and short meetings that make up much of our interactions on a day-to-day basis within our teams and our departments, both with our colleagues and our customers.

'Each interaction has an effect on us, both good and bad. The totality of these interactions during the course of an average week has a real effect on how we feel, how we perform and how we in turn treat others. The real test is being able to be the cause of quality conversation, even when what you want to give to those around you isn't what you get from them.

'We know that quality conversations are the basis for:

- Trusting relationships

- The ability to have a really valuable and challenging conversation

- Recognising effort in a way that has real impact

- Enabling true empowerment and ownership to occur

'Think for a moment about the number of people you've interacted with over the last month, both those more senior and those you perhaps have a responsibility for. How many would say that it was a positive experience for them? And how many of the people who've interacted with you have had a positive effect on you? These aren't trick questions, as the outcome of these interactions really does make a difference to how it feels to come to work each day.'

The billion-dollar quality conversation

'One of the biggest players in the construction and support services industry recently bought one of the other biggest players in the construction and support services industry. Know who? We know that the CEO of one of these businesses led the business from bankruptcy in 2011 to one of the most respected turnarounds in UK corporate history. At the time of writing, the ink of the deal is still wet as it was done in June 2015. The CEO began the journey in 2011 by *specifically focusing on building great relationships through quality conversations with all key stakeholders*, both within (people), and outside (customers, regulatory bodies, investors, community interest groups) the business. It worked: the business went on to win one of the largest ($1.09 billion) roadway maintenance contracts in Europe in 2014, all down to the art of listening and conversing.

'So what's the most precious commodity that no one has that much of? Yes, time. Everyone's diaries are manic these days. The great thing about quality conversations is that they don't require more time to be invested – if anything they can take less time. There are key 'set-play' moments in the diary, like team briefings, one-to-ones, and meetings that often play out a certain way because they've played out that way for ages. The trick is to use these current interaction/conversation opportunities a little differently by thinking about the impact we're making on others, and the impact others are having on us. Both can be changed and improved.'

Really Listen Summary Checklist: 10 Big Things

1. Make an effort to remember little details about people, as this can make a massive difference.

2. Concentrate on what people are saying rather than preparing what you are going to say next.

3. Don't finish people's sentences. It's annoying, and you might not get it right either.

4. To be truly listening, you can't be doing or thinking anything else at the same time.

5. Be mindful of creating the best possible environment to enable you to listen – take control of this.

6. Deep questioning and listening opens up a person's true personality, motivations and feelings.

7. Be aware of your body language to show positive clues that you are genuinely listening.

8. Taking relevant, timely action on what people have said is a great way to show that you heard them.

9. Not all your actions need to be known by others. Trust what feels right, and results will come.

10. And finally, don't invite suggestions if you can't or won't deliver the appropriate solutions.

CHAPTER 7:

BE SOCIABLE

'If you're not having fun, you're doing something wrong.'

Groucho Marx

Have fun

Back in the 1980s and 90s, before the global economic crisis turned the world on its axis, and before the true advent of smart technology and mobile working, corporate life often had a heavy social angle, both within and outside working hours.

As we all know, life isn't like that anymore – the corporate world has moved on in the last 20 years to an environment that is, typically, full of relentless pressure, stress, and a stream of tough decisions. There are almost no jobs left where people literally finish what needs doing, compared to the past where you would regularly clear your 'in-tray'. These days, the in-tray (or rather inbox) is always full. This constant level of pressure can become overwhelming for many employees, and they often crave a release valve to offset this mental squeeze.

Many try to find a personal release outside work, but this can be dangerous because the tendency can be to max out to extremes. As I covered in Chapter 2 ('Care for Others' – Wellbeing), my personal view is that a culture of extreme behaviours, be it adrenalin rushes, promiscuity, gambling, over-eating and obesity, binge drinking and heavy alcohol reliance, is in many cases a by-product of people using fixed time-bound pockets to escape and blot out the mental noise that they face from 9 to 5, or in many cases longer. The impact of this can be heavily counter-productive to subsequent performance in the workplace.

The good news is that there is actually a quick and immediate solution. It is simply to create an environment where *fun* is acceptable and, in fact, is encouraged. It doesn't have to be complicated. For example, everybody loves a game, so turning anything into a game is a sure fire way of building fun, but for this solution to be credible it *must* be led by the leadership of the company.

As leaders, if you don't ever appear to be having fun, or creating fun, or supporting situations where fun might be a by-product, then the prevailing culture you set is one where no employees feel they have permission to enjoy themselves or let go in any way. This leads to a culture where people's true personalities are suppressed, they behave in a very managed (unnatural) way, and there is almost no chance of interactions between people moving past first base.

Even worse, an environment where fun is not deemed to be acceptable inadvertently encourages the 'mood hoovers', 'energy vampires' and 'policy enforcers' to have a field day. Anyone having fun is considered to be mucking about, not taking things seriously, not having enough work to do, not realising how tough things are, not respecting how much pressure others are under. This is really sad, because in many cases having fun can provide the release valve that embeds an individual into the organisation, drives their engagement and performance, and actually prevents them holding out for the non-work binges of excitement and release.

I encourage you, as a leader, to create an environment where having fun is embraced and promoted. And that starts with you. Ask yourself the question 'When is the last time I had a proper, genuine, hearty laugh in work?' If you don't know, then you are taking life too seriously. Others will be aware of this, and are probably following your lead.

So, create opportunities for fun. Make it a priority, whether planned or spontaneous. People who work with or around you might not publicly thank you, but inside they will feel released from tension, and life will be put into perspective.

A major financial institution under an enormous amount of public and internal pressure during the banking crisis literally had to pick up their workforce, who were on their knees with stress and despair. In an initiative spearheaded by the CEO and HR Director, they made having fun one of their top three corporate priorities for the year. They spoke openly about how there was complete permission to do so. All people managers and leaders were encouraged (and rewarded) to create an environment for their people that was fun to be in at every opportunity. People loved it, and were so relieved. It was a smart organisational message, that many other companies have cottoned on to in recent years: business is serious, but we don't always have to be serious in the way we go about it.

Don't dodge non-work stuff

You will find quite a bit of rhetoric about the apparent need to draw the line between work and non-work, especially as you move into leadership. Courses on moving to leadership often highlight how you can't be one of the gang any more, and they encourage you to let go of past relationships and redefine them. Furthermore, never is a function under as much scrutiny as HR in terms of drawing clear boundaries between work and personal life.

So all in all, a low-risk leadership strategy would be to make the boundaries between work and personal life clearly defined, wouldn't it? Well, no, not any more. Hierarchy is dying. We live in a different dynamic world now, increasingly governed by your social standing and public rating and how much people approve of you rather than by any organisation level or position power. Some futurists even believe that social approval will replace money as the major global commodity in the next 100 years. It's a world increasingly full of 21-year-old CEOs and flat gradeless structures, and it's happening absolutely everywhere – even many government departments are investing in modernising the workplace in terms or structure and culture.

The danger is that many leaders, have gone too far the other way. They manage to justify opting out of being social, in particular for one of the following four reasons:

1. They are scared and worry about crossing the lines, so they avoid the risk.

2. They actually can't be bothered. Sometimes it's as simple as that.

3. They have been conditioned by working for previous leaders who haven't valued the caring, sociable side of leadership.

4. They don't fully understand the value of being sociable with people versus the in-tray.

In fact, participating in the social aspects of company life is disproportionately powerful for a leader. People typically feel valued and important if a leader finds the time to attend a lunch, a weekend BBQ, charity day, bowling evening, Santa's present giving – I could go on. It shows that the people *matter*, and there is a cause/purpose/higher calling greater than just commercial profitability that leads you to be involved and contribute more broadly. Great leaders of the future will regularly join in socially outside the boundaries of work, often in their personal time.

However, I will wave a red flag here – be very aware of how you act and the choices you make when you do attend these events. Bear in mind the following questions that others in attendance may be asking themselves:

- Are the managers and leaders really being sociable or are they standing in their usual little groups with each other, almost like an extension of a weekly management meeting?

- Are they genuinely letting go of their senior buddies and mingling with people from all levels and functions?

- What are their topics of conversation – are they focussed on work, or do they talk about what is important socially?

- Most importantly, are they talking or listening?

Perhaps have these thoughts as your own checklist for the next social event you attend, and add a few of your own by considering it from the attendees' viewpoint.

Being sociable also extends into your use of social media tools. Some of the most inspiring leaders of our time are those who have a deep and wide social footprint across the major applications such as Facebook, Twitter, LinkedIn, etc. Richard Branson is one of the most glowing examples. Regular exchanges of real-time data connect people (and customers) to leaders in a way that has never been possible before, and people really start feeling as if they know leaders as people, even as friends. However, a frightening statistic is that two thirds of UK CEOs are *still* avoiding having a social footprint for others to follow and connect with, and they are sadly missing out on an incredibly powerful collaboration tool. This attitude is not sustainable. The social media uprising will eventually overtake them unless they quickly bounce forward into the digital age and take a risk.

Get back to the floor

Quite simply, *this works*. Any effort from leadership to be seen empathising with the workforce by stepping into their shoes is usually well received. Interestingly, despite the increasingly high volume of information and TV programmes (e.g. *Undercover Boss*) showing all the benefits of leaders getting back to operational level, this is still one of the biggest things that leaders secretly try to avoid. In fact, it is probably only a close second to a requirement for public speaking, to which many leaders start feeling slightly sick at the thought.

The concept of getting back to the floor is hardly a revolutionary one. Take Leo Tolstoy, who was born in 1828 into an aristocratic Russian family that owned an estate and hundreds of serfs. The early life of the young count was raucous and violent, but he gradually weaned himself off his decadent lifestyle and rejected the conditioned beliefs of his background, adopting a radical, unconventional view of the world that shocked his peers. One such trait was his capacity to empathise by stepping into the shoes of people whose lives were vastly different from his own. In the 1860s, he not only adopted peasant dress, but began working alongside the labourers on his estate, ploughing the fields and repairing their homes with his own hands. In those days, such actions by a member of the nobility were nothing short of remarkable. Tolstoy believed you could never understand the reality of other people's lives unless you'd had a taste of it yourself. He was, without realising, trailblazing an alternative style of leadership, and it worked.

What 'getting back to the floor' means is broad in its definition. It is basically any effort by leaders to be visible in a face-to-face environment with employees who are typically either working at the front end or in the back office of the company or entity. In all cases the leaders are mixing with operational, administrative and/or service-oriented workers, or with customers.

At its most intense, it can for example mean a senior leader working for a few weeks as a shop assistant, and doing everything that the shop assistant would do. From these experiences, the leader can see the impact of their decisions through the lens of the customer and employee, and in many cases they already have the authority, or gift, to improve things immediately.

At its most basic, getting back to the floor can literally mean popping in on your front line, whatever that is – field workers, shops, back office departments – and stopping by a few people's work stations to say 'How are you doing?' And listening to the answer. Say 'Well done, keep going', and then move on.

So why is the act of being visible with the core workforce and customer base often avoided? There are many reasons I have come across. My challenge to each of the more regular excuses (below) is in italics - I am going to be blunt.

'I don't have enough time, there is too much to do, I can't justify it…'

Really? What can be more important to your current and future organisational success than improving the service to customers through engaged and motivated employees?

'I won't know what to say to the staff…'

As a recent book phenomenon says, 'Feel the fear and do it anyway!' Try starting with what the Queen does and ask people 'What do you do?' The conversation will go from there. Think of good, open questions. Be human, find common ground, build relationships by talking about things other than the job. Relax about it.

'I will look stupid if I can't help the customer, or if I can't do the employee's basic tasks…'

Not true. Customers and staff love the idea of seeing leaders being at the coal face. They watch the TV programmes. Just tell them what you are doing, and they will be lenient.

'I actually find the idea daunting. It's well out of my comfort zone…'

You are paid to lead, not hide, so get visible. The first time will be the hardest, and then, like a path well-trodden over time, the process gets easier and becomes normal, comfortable and enjoyable. (Yes, enjoyable. You will actively want to do it.)

'I am worried they will have tough questions that I can't answer…'

You won't know unless you try it. There really is no downside. Even if the questions are tough, at least you will know the key issues on the frontline.

And finally, there is one reason that very much exists but will rarely, if ever, be vocalised:

'It is beneath me. I am far too important.'

If you know people like this, or spot a little bit of this in your own mentality, a big step forward is to start challenging it, and maybe try some of the other options available or encourage others to do so. They will thank you for it in the long run.

A colleague of mine shared a story about a personal experience with a boss who perhaps fitted the 'superiority complex' category . When my colleague joined a pharmaceutical plant in Liverpool in his mid-30s as a middle manager, he insisted on doing something that nobody had ever done: he spent his entire first week working for one full day at each of the five different production plants. He explained how the respect he gained from this approach was incredible, as were the looks of amazement on the faces of the staff. He used the process to find out about their views of the company – what was good and what could be better – and was horrified to find out that nobody he spoke to could name the Managing Director . (The company employed just 350 people, and the MD was based on site.) As my colleague said, 'You couldn't make it up', although sadly this is not an isolated example of a world that a new generation of *Loving Leaders* won't even recognise as a leadership style.

As I was writing this book, another great example of leaders getting their hands dirty came to light, involving the Operational Lead for JT's £50m Gigabit Fibre Broadband installation project. (Jersey will soon have the fastest broadband speeds in the world, which we are all very excited about.) I asked Paul, the very modest leader in question, to explain what happened, 'I had spent the afternoon out visiting the installation teams under one of the field supervisors. As is always the case, if I am not doing a scheduled audit on any of the teams, I dress exactly the same as the installers, with safety boots, work trousers, branded JT polo shirt and high visibility jacket. We had spent a reasonable amount of time with the team on the first install working out the solution, and had got physically involved on the next team's job on the (very mucky) cable run.

'Towards the end of the day we got back to the office to see one of the new installers sorting out his tools and new van. I introduced myself as Paul, and he said "Alright mate", or words to that effect. It wasn't until the new installer's supervisor came over and said to him, "So you've met the big boss then" that it registered that I was one of the leadership team. On understanding this, the installer was shocked that I was dressed the same as him and more than a little dirty from the activities of the afternoon. His comment was "Blimey, I never saw the senior management in the field in the UK, never mind getting their hands dirty doing the job like us."

'For me, understanding the complexities of what the installers have to deal with and actually doing the job with them means I am able not only to appreciate what they do, but also visualise the problems they are having, hopefully increasing the problem solving. Along with this, the installers understand I know their job and they can't pull the wool over my eyes. I will come out and see them at any time, and if push came to shove I would always help if required.'

CASE STUDY: Carole Woodhead, CEO of Hermes Parcelnet

Carole was awarded the highly acclaimed 'People Focussed CEO of the Year' at the 2015 HR Distinction Awards. This is no mean feat when you consider the scale of her logistics challenge: in the UK alone, Hermes handles a mind-boggling 200 million-plus parcels each year. This includes fulfilling major logistics contracts with online retail brands such as Next Directory, ASOS, Tesco, John Lewis, Debenhams and Arcadia Group, with a customer promise that up to 95% of parcels are delivered first time. As Hermes Parcelnet enters is sixth consecutive year of double digit growth in one of the toughest industries around, I wanted to find out more about what Carole does to engage her people and inspire them to achieving such great things.

Carole's leadership passions sit firmly in showing a strong sociable side to her character – be it through communication, proactively interacting with people, approachability or staff engagement. Carole prides herself on being able to bring the business challenges to life in a way that people understand and connect with, and she embeds this directly through talking to the business in a simple and inspiring way. As Carole puts it, 'I put the edges and lines to the jigsaw, and leave plenty of blank space for people to decide how they want to fill it in.'

Building on this, a key leadership strength that Carole prides herself on is *visibility* at the coal face of her organisation. Her mantra is to 'be there' with the workforce, and during the peak period of deliveries Carole manages to visit at least 20 of the 30 main depots over a two-month period. She uses these visits to reinforce messages and priorities (such as her *Ambition2017* plans), and for listening to what key issues are being faced by her workforce. Then she does all she can to help them achieve their key targets.

Carole uses multiple methods of media to communicate and engage with staff, such as videos, podcasts and monthly pulse information, all of which are opportunities for her to pass on her passion, energy and focus around the business. She has neatly simplified the strategy in an effort to get the coal face workers focussed on the right things through a 'Road to Success' storyboard.

Carole also creates plenty of time for fun at Hermes, and instils a work-hard, play-hard culture. At the end of the day, she says that she doesn't take herself too seriously and this rubs off on others. At Hermes, Carole leads by example, making it clear that it is completely acceptable to have a good blow out and let your hair down, and she certainly has an engaging human side. She is very authentic in sharing her life and experiences with others in a non-hierarchical fashion. A clear case in point is a recent management conference that was run in the format of TV gameshow *Blankety Blank*, and culminated in a 3am (very well behaved!) finish in the bar.

Carole has a firm belief that at the end of the day, everything is all about people dealing with people. She invests in face-to-face relationships to drive levels of trust with all stakeholders, and it clearly pays off. Interestingly, Carole doesn't actively manage any type of social media footprint. For her it's all about being present, either in person, or through videos, rather than blogs. When we debated this point further, Carole identified that she may need to consider doing something soon as the communication tools and preferences of her workforce and customers change, especially with the next generations. That said, Carole is certainly an exponent of the fact that nothing beats a good bit of face-to-face communication if you want to build relationships, and her workforce certainly echoes this through the endorsements that led to Carole winning her much coveted award. So a learning point for leaders who are heavily leveraging social media tools is to be careful not to allow these channels to replace face-to-face methods completely.

EXPERT VIEW: Sue Stoneman, CEO of NKD Learning

NKD Learning (www.nkd.co.uk) is one of my favourite HR consultancies, helping people fall in love with their brands and become walking-talking adverts for their organisation. NKD unleashes the power of emotion in organisations, the result being millions of engaged employees and customers. Having read the content of *Loving Leadership*, CEO Sue Stoneman felt that the themes in 'Be Sociable' shared a lot of the philosophy that NKD is run on.

'At NKD we are often asked to help organisations with large-scale cultural change programmes. One of our starting points for this work is to ask leaders to tell us about the non-work culture, as this gives us a unique insight into how they view culture and how hard the project will be. The results are very telling, and can be broadly broken down into three areas:

- The parent leader – "I cramp their style"; "They have more fun without me"

- The self-important leader – "I am too busy"; "I don't have time"

- The cultural leader – "I love this job"; "My people make this job fun"

'Culture is often said to be what happens when you are *not* in the room, but in our view at NKD, culture should be what happens whether you are in the room or out of it.

'Taking a backseat in your company's culture is a quick-fire way to organisational mediocrity; it distances you from your frontline and from your customers. It also excuses you from the human side of work, and that sounds, well, er…shit.

'Say on your death bed, "I really do wish I had spent more time at work" and be one of the few to mean it!' We talk more with Sue in Chapter 8.

Be sociable Summary Checklist: 10 Big Things

1. Get socially involved with your team outside of work, and don't talk about work – it works.

2. Hierarchy is dying – the old days of leaders distancing themselves from staff is dying with it.

3. If you are not being as sociable as you could, take a look in the mirror and ask yourself why.

4. You need to create and maintain an engaging social media footprint to win hearts and minds.

5. Create lots of opportunities in and out of work for people to have fun and enjoy themselves.

6. Set the tone by letting yourself have fun so others see that you don't take yourself too seriously.

7. Make time in your day to walk around amongst other teams and departments. Be a visible leader.

8. Get your hands dirty; don't ask anyone to do something that you wouldn't actually do yourself.

9. *Remember*: without happy staff, you won't have happy customers. No-one will be happy.

10. Everybody loves a game, so create opportunities to turn tasks and situations into games.

CHAPTER 8:

PAINT PICTURES

*'Every now and then one paints a picture
that seems to have opened a door and
serves as a stepping stone to other things.'*

Pablo Picasso

Turn your word vision into a picture

Our day-to-day actions and responses are guided to a large extent by our major sensory inputs, namely visual (sight, how we see the world), audio (sound, what we hear) and kinaesthesia (gut feelings, how we touch and feel emotions). Researchers have shown that, on average, when we make decisions, we base 45% on our visual inputs and 40% on our gut feelings, leaving a mere 15% based on what we hear (words and sounds). Therefore that any word statement will only ever be a maximum of 15% successful.

So many opportunities to inspire a workforce are missed when we use words, and only words, to try and create a call to action. Visions that only ever exist in the written word are in many cases a complete waste of time, no matter how beautifully 'word-smithed', because of the basic preferences with which humans process information and make decisions. In fact, by their very nature, visions cannot actually be words and sentences. For something to be a vision, it must be a representation of what success looks like, of what the words actually mean, i.e. an *image*.

Consider the following all-too-familiar types of apparent vision statements:

- 'We will create double digit growth every year for the next five years'

- 'We will be a consistent top-tier law firm, specialising in corporate finance'

- 'Our building blocks of success are profitability, margin growth and process optimisation'

Blah, blah, blah, yawn! This is doomed never to win any hearts and minds. It may be a nice reminder for the executives and their long-term incentive schemes in the lofty boardrooms, and sounds good if you are shareholder, I suppose, but that's all.

What about the employees? What about the people who actually make the company the success that it is? Do these words inspire them? No. Do they want to hear about cost control and optimisation? No. Do they really care what the revenue and EBITDA projection is? On the whole, no, they don't. Companies far too often try and excite the workers with what excites them, and wonder why others don't come on the bus with them. They don't because this is not the life or set of values that many people have chosen, and even if it was, it still doesn't conjure up a particularly exciting destination or direction of travel.

The majority of people care about something far simpler and more compelling – something that they can *picture*. They want a vision. An inspiring image. Something aspirational. An exciting destination. A better place to create, build a legacy, make a visible difference, make people happy.

So what does that look like? How will your team/company make a visible difference and how can this be visualised and brought to life? In a picture. In a diagram. Whatever you like. Now you are talking...

If we want to win hearts and minds quickly, let's create a *picture* of the vision.

David Powell, inspirational speaker and author of *Spirit Intelligence*, agrees. He says, 'When communicating purpose, the picture is indeed worth the proverbial thousand words, and graphical visions and pictures of the envisaged success horizon are very powerful in improving communication. Witness the powerful effect of the picture of the earth taken by the Apollo astronauts from the moon. We all got that our spaceship is a tiny island in the blackness of space.'

This concept has also been a fundamental pillar of major FTSE100 employee-branding programmes driven by Sue Stoneman, CEO of NKD Learning, who says:

'"A picture paints a thousand words" is an oft used expression, but it is also one that is all too often forgotten by business leaders in the day-to-day running of their business. Organisations invest huge amounts of money and resources in getting their advertising and merchandising to entice customers to invest in their products and services yet fail to use the same psychology to engage their own people. For most organisations their vision and values become paragraphs of well-meaning corporate jargon left in an induction pack gathering dust in the bottom of a drawer.

'In today's world where employees are ever more interested in the purpose of their role, being able to paint the best cultural picture and then live it is fast becoming *the* point of differentiation. Powerful emotive imagery should be deployed inwardly as much as it should be on your potential customers. In a connected world, brand has become interdependent with culture, and as such demands more thought than all but a few are giving it.'

When you are creating icons and images, remember that it's really important to appeal to the desired audience. The images need to be meaningful and powerful to them. In fact, I would encourage you to go a step further and let the whole team, or even the wider workforce, contribute to creating the pictorial image of the vision, rather than trying to influence them to be inspired by something that only you have dreamt up.

So, no time like the present – I challenge you to get hold of any strategies, visions, purposes and statements, and if there is nothing visual associated with them, you know what to do. Good luck!

Draw what you mean

Communicating spontaneously in pictures or diagrams is incredibly powerful. Whenever you are discussing something that has multiple views or outputs, never be afraid to get up and start drawing it for all participants to see, even just a couple of boxes with an arrow from A to B. You will be amazed what this simple act does. People's creative juices are fired. Contributions increase. Debate warms. Solutions are raised. Pros and cons are debated. And best of all, the image sticks. Everyone will remember the chart/pillars/diagram/graph/process map, even if they can't remember all the detail. Try it. Daily. There is no down side. (Remember to rub off anything career limiting or controversial afterwards – but take a photo first!).

I worked for one inspiring leader who found it almost impossible to resist getting up and scribbling on his whiteboard or flipchart when we were in problem solving/ debate mode, which was daily. I remember it because so often it helped to break down and simplify a problem and focus on what was important. But he was the exception. So many leaders don't do this – in fact, there seems to be an invisible grade that is reached by certain senior people whereby standing up with a thick pen and doing a bit of facilitation and brainstorming becomes uncool. Maybe they feel it's below them, or maybe they lack the skills.

Whatever the reason, if your communication exchange with people around you is only ever in the form of words, whether written or spoken, you will never get close to unleashing the true power and results that sit there, latently bursting to come out as soon as people are given a pictorial invitation to do so.

And clearly, a whiteboard can be substituted by any other means of visual communication – flip charts, online presentation tools, or simply drawing your ideas out on a piece of paper. The point is that language is open to interpretation, and doesn't always leave a lasting memory. Visuals are much more definite as everyone is seeing the same picture. They might use different words to describe exactly what the picture says, but the point is that you will achieve greater levels of alignment by bringing words to life through pictures, charts and imagery.

The other great power of pictures rather than words is that they transcend boundaries, cultures, languages, and indeed any assumptions, generalisations or preconceptions people have with certain words.

This became particularly clear to me when I consulted with a workforce in the British Virgin Islands over a new and exciting set of brand values for a global organisation. One of the defining areas that we had almost settled on, having consulted seven other jurisdictions, was about building *strength* in the brand. However, the British Virgin Islands representatives said that this simply made no sense to them – only a *person* could have strength, not a brand, so they gave feedback that this would not inspire the British Virgin Islands workforce. In fact, it would confuse them. We subsequently changed the wording and descriptors to focus on how globally recognised and admired we could help the brand to become. However, in hindsight, had there been an image that depicted what we meant by a strong global brand (which we were calling 'strength'), this issue would perhaps never have come up.

Use memorable images

In classic communication and learning theory you will have learned that, allegedly, the world is a mixture of people who are visual, audio or kinaesthetic. The truth is that everyone has a mix of these, but typically has a slight leaning towards one rather than the others. For example, you will hear people say, 'I'm a visual person, draw what you mean', or 'I'm an audio person, explain what that means in your own words'.

However, when it comes to visual imagery, whether it's your natural learning preference or not, *everybody* can anchor a deep feeling of connection. Pictures are the most powerful call to action, evoking emotions that words and feelings can't convey. The more that you do to anchor memorable relevant images alongside delivering results, the better chance you will have of aligning the efforts of all the people around you towards a compelling vision of the future.

Whenever you use visuals, make sure they are beautiful. Never rush the design or choice of a visual element. Don't just use something found within 10 seconds from Clip Art. Take time to choose a stunning photograph or image that brings to life what you are saying. If someone is helping you with your leadership communications, make sure that they reflect your standards and personality in the imagery used.

The advertising and marketing industry has some of the best success by creating lasting emotional images that shape people's views on a particular brand, product or service. By having an image of the experience that is being created, you can get customers and employees excited by the same vision, and as a leader it is so much easier to drive cultural alignment.

As Shaun Smith touched on in the chapter on 'Magic Moments', one of the best successes that Smith & Co was involved in was Premier Inn's 'Great Night's Sleep' promise, which their entire strategy hangs off. For me, the image of Lenny Henry snoozing on a Premier Inn bed perfectly captures the power of visuals to drive this understanding, and what is important becomes very clear to all employees.

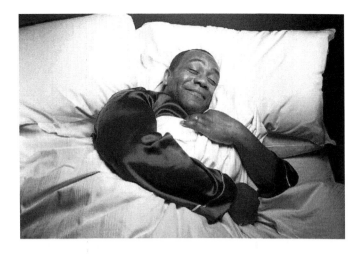

Exactly the same concept applies when you are trying to rally people around the achievement of any objective, task or vision. It all becomes so much clearer when you can *see* it. As a leader, this is such a major tool at your disposal, and if it doesn't come naturally to you, ensure you have talented people around you who can really bring your vision to life through images.

CASE STUDY: Martin Cooper, Finance Director at BAE Systems

In 2012 BAE Systems brought together 3,500 people from diverse heritages to form Maritime Services. This created a once-in-a-generation opportunity to work with customers to help create a modern workforce to support a modern navy based at a modern naval base. At the helm of this major change was Martin Cooper, Finance and IT Director.

A business transformation strategy was developed to invest in people, tools, systems, processes and infrastructure. This improved sustainability, optimised performance and drove down cost. The leadership team recognised that to engage and inspire staff to be up for the journey, they needed to take the strategy out of Word documents and PowerPoint slides, and bring it to life.

That was the thinking behind the approach to employee engagement which led to the creation of the Maritime Services' 'Rich Picture'. The guts of the picture started with data collection through employee roadshows where feedback was gathered from more than 350 staff, leaders, trade unions and, importantly, customers as to what the future could look like if the strategy was realised. This input was used to develop a compelling pictorial representation of their business strategy and the key challenges ahead.

By working with Delta7 and following their process, the Rich Picture became a visual dialogue facilitation tool that encouraged engaging conversations about the business's change journey, creating two-way dialogue at all levels in the organisation to listen to employees' views and feedback. This established that change and strategy realisation is everyone's responsibility, not just that of the leadership team, managers or a few business change agents. The programme, which has advanced the staff engagement journey, has enabled Maritime Services to continue to drive its strategy, make everyone realise what role they have to play in the business's future and create a constant reference tool to keep the business aligned during change journeys, which are always difficult.

As Martin explained, 'It's a common mistake in management committees and boards to create a strategic plan that is understood and agreed to be very clear and powerful in the eyes of those people who created it. In many cases, that is because it involved a good cerebral debate in its creation, and ultimately something challenging and aspirational has been written down which would clearly drive the company's

Maritime Services rich picture is courtesy of Delta 7

growth and profits, typically to the benefit of everyone around that table.

'Unfortunately', continued Martin, 'that doesn't wash with others in the organisation. They get stimulated and connected through different things in life, and a different angle is needed to get them as interested in the company strategy as the leaders are. This can be achieved through the power of a picture explaining the destination but allowing interpretation by different people. Furthermore, images stick and promote deeper conversation than a bunch of words, and it is this concept that drove us to create the Rich Picture to engage the whole of Maritime Services in the creation of a new model of operation with great success.

'So, with great excitement, the Rich Picture was unveiled at the 2013 Maritime Services Leadership Conference which marked a true turning point in the company's direction: a shared sense of purpose was evident within the room. Maritime Services then skilled up over 100 "Story Sharers" who passionately shared the message across all 3,500 staff within four months, and in the 2014 staff survey there was a clear increase in knowledge and understanding of the business strategy, the need and desire to maintain high levels of employee engagement, and employees understanding their role in delivering the collective strategy and business imperatives. Story sharing has continued for all new joiners at BAE to reinforce the message.'

EXPERT VIEW: Darren Briggs, MD of Flametree Communication

Darren has nearly 25 years of global experience working at chief executive and board level in internal communications. He has had an enviable corporate career in HR, marketing and corporate communication functions spanning some of the world's best-known brands and most fast-changing companies, including British Airways, Microsoft, Nike, PepsiCo and Vodafone. He is a well-known expert in leadership communication and has extensive international executive communication coaching experience, delivered through his company, Flametree Communication.

Darren found that the 'Paint Pictures' chapter captured many elements of things he has seen succeed in his own experience, and he referred to a particularly powerful example as follows:

'Aristotle's theory of rhetoric from over 2,000 years ago provides leaders with the framework they need to persuade and influence people. In my experience, most leaders are comfortable talking about facts, figures and data; typically being more rational and logical with their argument. Sadly, they are less comfortable with appealing to people at an emotional level by painting a compelling mental picture of what they want people to do. Truly inspirational leaders can do both of these things brilliantly.

'I remember working several years ago for London 2012 and the London Organising Committee for the Olympic Games (LOCOG). As my client, I had the privilege to work with Lord Coe concerning the need to develop a compelling vision for the people who were working on the delivery of the Olympics. I recall an early conversation when Coe explained that he recognised early in the process that different people had a different picture of success for the Games – for some it was about winning gold medals, for others it was about building world-class sporting facilities.

'When we finally brought the LOCOG team together to introduce the vision and values for the LOCOG organisation, Coe talked about why he was so driven by the London Games and how he was focussed on leaving a legacy for a future generation of athletes to emerge. By using facts to persuade people of what could be possible, he then painted a very personal picture of how he viewed success, and this couldn't fail in influencing people to be part of his ambition to deliver a Games that the entire country would be proud of.'

Paint Pictures Summary Checklist: 10 Big Things

1. Never rely just on words for an inspiring vision, it must have an image associated with it.

2. Visuals are powerful where they paint a destination of what the future could look like.

3. Take opportunities to explain what you are trying to say in a picture or diagram.

4. The more inspiring and memorable the picture, the deeper the emotional engagement.

5. Always have the audience in mind – tailor the imagery to things that light their fire, not yours.

6. Use pictures to simplify complex discussions and messages – let others interpret.

7. Encourage story-telling around images and pictures; stimulate debate.

8. Be proactive in meetings with the use of whiteboards and flip charts to facilitate discussions.

9. For important messages, invest time and money creating beautiful and memorable images.

10. Encourage others to engage more through imagery, and pass this technique on.

CHAPTER 9:

MAKING IT STICK

Firstly, congratulations for reaching the final chapter – you are already in a top percentile of readers of developmental business books worldwide. Why? Because millions of business books are sold to people who never reach the end, myself included. I have several books sitting idly on my Kindle, with good intentions on my part, but they stay overlooked. I may have liked the title, the theme of the back page, maybe some of the names in the case studies, but even so, something stops me getting to the end. It may be priorities. Quality. Whatever it is, I don't quite make it.

Even though you have got to the end, the hard work is still to be done. Advice is only really going to help you if you drive the changes. Finishing a business tools book is a bit like finishing a training course. Even if you enjoyed it immensely, it is only the ability to translate the learning rapidly into different repeatable behaviours that will drive change. There is an old adage that says, 'Do something 100 times and then decide whether it's sustainable and beneficial'. So, with this in mind, how are you going to make anything stick that has resonated in this book?

A good starting point is to drill down on what really matters at this point in your life and career by an honest assessment of the things that will make the biggest difference right now.

Exercise: where to focus your energy

Turn back to the start of this book. You honestly and objectively rated where you were against the 8 powerful techniques. Fill in where you are now below and add figures to illustrate where you *want* to be (**DESIRED**), then the gap between the two, and finally rank the priority from highest (**A**) to lowest (**H**). The highest won't necessarily be the factor with the largest gap, but it might be. Choose no more than three (**A, B, C**) to start working on – even less is fine.

Remember: score yourself out of 10 where 0 is you don't ever do it, 10 is that you do it all the time.

Your name: ....   **Date:** ....

Give Trust	NOW	DESIRED	GAP	PRIORITY ....
Care for Others	NOW	DESIRED	GAP	PRIORITY ....
Be Vulnerable	NOW	DESIRED	GAP	PRIORITY ....
Shine a Light	NOW	DESIRED	GAP	PRIORITY ....
Create Magic Moments	NOW	DESIRED	GAP	PRIORITY ....
Really Listen	NOW	DESIRED	GAP	PRIORITY ....
Be Sociable	NOW	DESIRED	GAP	PRIORITY ....
Paint Pictures	NOW	DESIRED	GAP	PRIORITY ....

Additional personal notes/actions

Priority A

Priority B

Priority C

And finally, to reinforce the points that these are techniques that everyone should work on, and that nobody is perfect, here are the scores of the author. Needless to say, I am already working hard on my 'Really Listen' and 'Be Vulnerable' skills this year.

Author's scores as of October 2015

	NOW	DESIRED	GAP	PRIORITY
Give Trust	NOW ... 7 ...	DESIRED ... 8 ...	GAP ... 1 ...	PRIORITY ....
Care for Others	NOW ... 7 ...	DESIRED ... 9 ...	GAP ... 2 ...	PRIORITY ... C ...
Be Vulnerable	NOW ... 6 ...	DESIRED ... 9 ...	GAP ... 3 ...	PRIORITY ... A ...
Shine a Light	NOW ... 8 ...	DESIRED ... 9 ...	GAP ... 1 ...	PRIORITY ....
Create Magic Moments	NOW ... 8 ...	DESIRED ... 9 ...	GAP ... 1 ...	PRIORITY ....
Really Listen	NOW ... 6 ...	DESIRED ... 9 ...	GAP ... 3 ...	PRIORITY ... B ...
Be Sociable	NOW ... 7 ...	DESIRED ... 8 ...	GAP ... 1 ...	PRIORITY ....
Paint Pictures	NOW ... 9 ...	DESIRED ... 9 ...	GAP ... 0 ...	PRIORITY ....

Not all at once

As I hinted at in the opening comments of the book, I do not believe there is a magic knock-them-dead formula for powerful leadership. There is a reason why I have suggested 8 powerful techniques that are often *missed*, the language clearly being to suggest that there are a lot of skills, techniques, styles and approaches (hundreds in fact) that are *not* missed. These other skills can be equally valid, and are part of the make-up of many good leaders' strengths and competencies.

Furthermore, different types of leadership roles require different styles and approaches, so it is very important for you to tailor your approach to the situation in hand.

So, if you have identified with more than two or three of the eight in the book, be kind to yourself and just try to do one at a time. Don't change too many things at once, because:

- You won't know which ones are making the biggest difference

- You will put yourself under pressure as these things probably don't come naturally to you or you would be doing them already

- You might scare people a little, and blow your cover of quietly improving your leadership quality

In summary: paradoxes and truisms

This short (and more philosophical) list was added after I felt that the book was complete. I reflected on some very powerful paradoxes and truisms that have come to light throughout the observations, theories and case studies covered. I hope they will serve as a useful leadership compass and something to reflect on as you prepare to act in future situations.

1. The best leaders delegate responsibility and actually let others do the leading.

2. Showing your weaknesses can be a major strength.

3. The more you try to control creativity, the more you constrain it.

4. To care for others is one of the most commercial behaviours that you can display.

5. Listening is a far greater communication skill than speaking.

6. The most inspiring leaders are often understated and will avoid the limelight.

7. The safer you try and play things, the bigger the risk you are often creating.

8. The more you exercise your power, the weaker you tend to appear.

9. If you don't take yourself too seriously, people will take you more seriously.

10. The smallest acts of kindness can have the biggest impact on others.

And finally, good luck

So, that's it. Simple. Over to you, and wishing you all the best in your quest to be a better leader, a better manager, a better person – whatever your mission is. Perhaps you will encourage the people who lead you to practise a few of these techniques a little more often as well.

I am always interested to hear from people who need a career boost, in particular from ambitious HR professionals and those in early-to-mid career stages with designs on being an inspiring future leader in their field.

I offer out-of-hours private career coaching, and if you want to ask me anything, I am very happy to be contacted via:

- email (richardjsummerfield@hotmail.com)

- Twitter (@rjsumm)

- LinkedIn (uk.linkedin.com/in/ richardsummerfieldjersey)

References and sources of Inspiration

- Best Companies www.b.co.uk

- UK HR Directors Business Summit www.hrevent.com

- *Water off a Duck's Back* – Jon Lavelle

- *The Speed of Trust* – Stephen M.R. Covey

- The Global Growth Institute, Wayne Clarke, www.the-ggi.com

- *The Road Less Travelled* – M. Scott Peck

- *Drive: the surprising truth about what motivates us* – Daniel H. Pink

- *Leading Change* – John P. Kotter

- thepeoplelikeyou.org Damien Clarkson

- *Bold: How to be Brave in Business and Win* – Shaun Smith

- *The Language of Leaders* – Kevin Murray

- *On Leadership* – Allan Leighton

- *The Art of Possibility* – Zander & Zander

- *Start with Why* – Steven Sinek

- David Powell., Spirit Intelligence, www.spirit-intelligence.com

- Richard Branson – Twitter feeds, articles, various interviews

- Graeme Codrington, www.tomorrowtoday.com

- Neville Pritchard, CEO HR in Flow

- Arianna Huffington @ huffingtonpost.com

- Steve Peters, The Chimp Paradox, www.chimpmanagement.com

- Darren Briggs, www.flametreecommunication.co.uk

- David Novak, www.yum.com

- Carole Woodhead, www.hermesworld.com

- Hoption, C., Barling, J., Turner, N. (2013). "'It's not you, it's me': transformational leadership and self-deprecating humor'. *Leadership & Organization Development Journal*, 34(1), 4 – 19

- www.forbes.com

- www.brenebrown.com

Corporate Logo

About the Author

Richard Summerfield is currently a Group HR Director and Board Member of JT (a high growth telecoms firm), Fellow of the CIPD (Chartered Institute of Personnel & Development), accredited career coach, qualified psychometric tester, industry speaker and commentator, HR Awards judge, and a recent double finalist at the 2013 UK CIPD Awards and the 2015 UK HR Distinction Awards. Richard's big passion is to create a better working environment for everyone, thereby giving people a greater chance of feeling happy, valued, giving their best, and reaching their full potential.